Home Workshop Series

QUICK & EASY
WOODWORKING PROJECTS

By the Editors of *WORKBENCH* Magazine

COPYRIGHT 1995 KC PUBLISHING, INC.

All rights reserved. No part of this work may be reproduced without written permission from the publisher, except by a reviewer who may quote short passages in a review with appropriate credits.

Instructions have been carefully checked for accuracy. The publisher, however, cannot be responsible for human error or misinterpretation of directions.

Attention Schools and Business Firms:
KC PUBLISHING books are available at quantity discounts for bulk purchases for education, business or sales promotion use. For more information call our Book Department at (816) 531-5730.

Printed in the United States of America

Library of Congress Cataloguing-in-Publication Data

QUICK & EASY WOODWORKING PROJECTS

By the Editors of *WORKBENCH* Magazine

ISBN: 0-86675-018-5

TABLE OF CONTENTS

Introduction	2
Color Previews of Projects	3

Furniture and Storage Projects — 13

3 CD Racks	14
3 Magazine Racks	20
Coat Rack	24
Fisherman's Wader Rack	26
Coffee Mug Tree	28
Knife Block With Cutting Board	32
Necklace Hanger	35
Tie Rack	36
Shelves to Go	38
Newspaper Recycling Bin	40
Knock-Down Table	42
Tile-Top Plant Stand	44

Projects for the Home Office — 49

Notepad Holder	50
Desktop File	52
Pencil Box	53
Bookends	55
Note Holder	56
Message Center	58
Plywood Wastebasket	60

Decorative Items — 63

Hanging Quilt Rack	64
Hexagonal Plant Trivet	66
Plant Ornaments	69
Octagonal Clocks	70
Picture Frames	73
Lathe-Turned Ornaments	76
Country Wall Hanging	80

Projects for Outdoors — 83

Firewood Rack/Plant Stand	84
House Marker	86
Southwest Planter Box	88
Boot/Shoe Scraper	90
Wooden Doormat	92
Garden Cart	94
Folding Lawn Chair	96
Berry Box	99

Kids' Stuff — 103

Toy Catapult	104
Decoupage Puzzle Blocks	106
Alphabet Shelf	108
Bewildering Blocks	110
Rubber Band Block Toy	112
Schoolhouse Blackboard	114

INTRODUCTION

Maybe you've been wanting to take up woodworking but haven't known where to start. Or perhaps it's been your hobby for years, but you just don't have enough time to build large, complicated pieces of furniture. Whatever your reasons for picking up this book, you'll find plenty of projects inside to keep you busy and give you a sense of accomplishment.

The simple designs in *Quick & Easy Woodworking Projects* are the perfect way for beginners to get their feet wet. More experienced craftsmen should be able to build any of the projects in just a few hours and may even develop ways to mass-produce them. The projects are ideal to give as gifts or sell at crafts fairs, but many are so useful you'll want to keep them for yourself.

The editors would like to thank the following people for their contributions to *Quick & Easy Woodworking Projects*: David Ashe, David Bayard, Richard Dettman, Steve Gilbert, Barbara Guyette, Gene and Katie Hamilton, Robert N. Hoffman, Harry E. Hunter, Terrance L. McFetridge, Kenn Oberrecht, Bernie Pfaff, Martha Pooley, Tom Sandbakken, Matt Scherrer, Dave Stewart, Melvin R. Thacher and Richard Wallace for the design and construction of many of the projects; Laurie Chipman and Eugene Thompson for their technical drawings and Al Surratt for his photos.

3
FURNITURE AND STORAGE PROJECTS

Coat Rack
Page 24

3 CD Racks
Page 14

3 Magazine Racks   Page 20

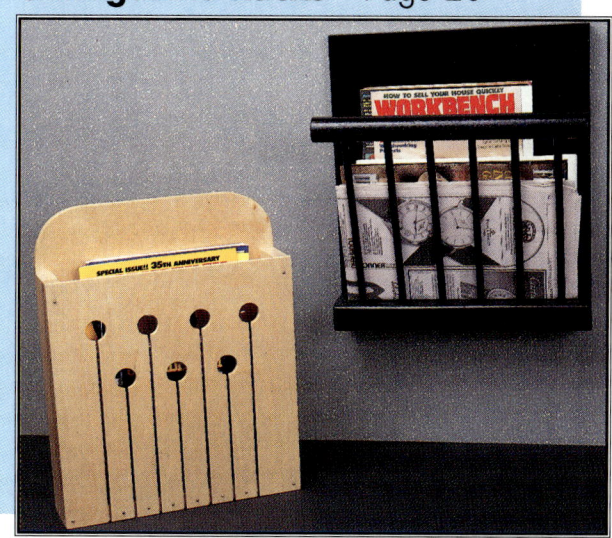

4
FURNITURE AND STORAGE PROJECTS

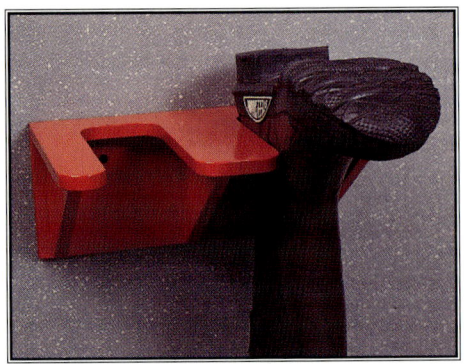

Fisherman's Wader Rack
Page 26

Necklace Hanger Page 35

Tie Rack   Page 36

Coffee Mug Tree   Page 28

**Knife Block
With Cutting Board**
Page 32

FURNITURE AND STORAGE PROJECTS

Shelves to Go
Page 38

Tile-Top Plant Stand
Page 44

Newspaper Recycling Bin
Page 40

Knock-Down Table   Page 42

6
PROJECTS FOR THE HOME OFFICE

Desktop File   Page 52   **Bookends**   Page 55

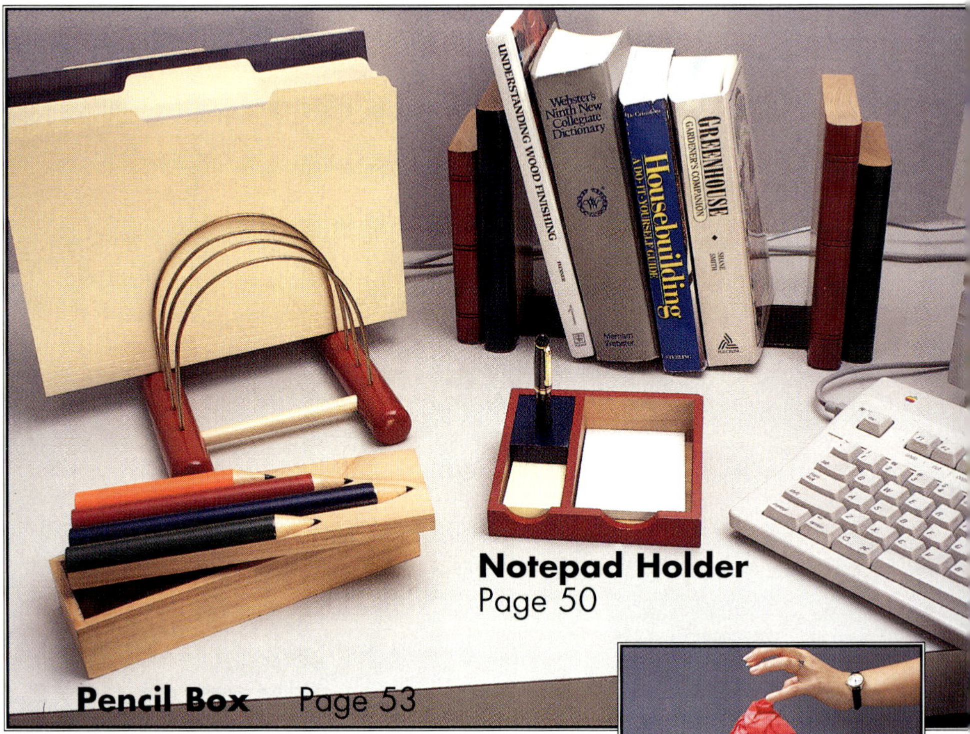

Notepad Holder
Page 50

Pencil Box   Page 53

Note Holder
Page 56

Message Center
Page 58

Plywood Wastebasket
Page 60

7
DECORATIVE ITEMS

Hanging Quilt Rack   Page 64

Plant Ornaments
Page 69

Hexagonal Plant Trivet
Page 66

Octagonal Clocks
Page 70

Picture Frames
Page 73

DECORATIVE ITEMS

Lathe-Turned Ornaments Page 76

Country Wall Hanging
Page 80

PROJECTS FOR OUTDOORS

House Marker
Page 86

Firewood Rack/ Plant Stand
Page 84

Southwest Planter Box
Page 88

PROJECTS FOR OUTDOORS

Boot/Shoe Scraper
Page 90

Berry Box   Page 99

Wooden Doormat
Page 92

Folding Lawn Chair
Page 96

Garden Cart
Page 94

KIDS' STUFF

Toy Catapult Page 104

Alphabet Shelf
Page 108

Decoupage Puzzle Blocks
Page 106

Bewildering Blocks
Page 110

Rubber Band Block Toy
Page 112

Schoolhouse Blackboard
Page 114

11
Quick & Easy

12
Quick & Easy

Quick & Easy
FURNITURE AND STORAGE PROJECTS

Quick & Easy

3 CD RACKS

White plastic dividers make it easy to slide in CD jewel boxes and allow you to use the rack horizontally or vertically. The CDs protrude slightly so you can grasp the edges.

The three racks shown on the following pages are simple and inexpensive to make, and they're more attractive than the plastic towers sold in stores.

1 SIMPLE, VERSATILE

The rack shown above holds 20 CDs and can be positioned vertically or horizontally. You can adapt the basic design to make longer racks, stacking racks, two-sided racks and many other variations.

The rack is made from readily available materials: 1/2-in. Baltic birch for the sides, 3/4-in.-dia. dowels for the supports, 3/32-in. white plastic for the dividers and 1/8-in. clear plastic for the stop. However, you can make

15
FURNITURE AND STORAGE PROJECTS

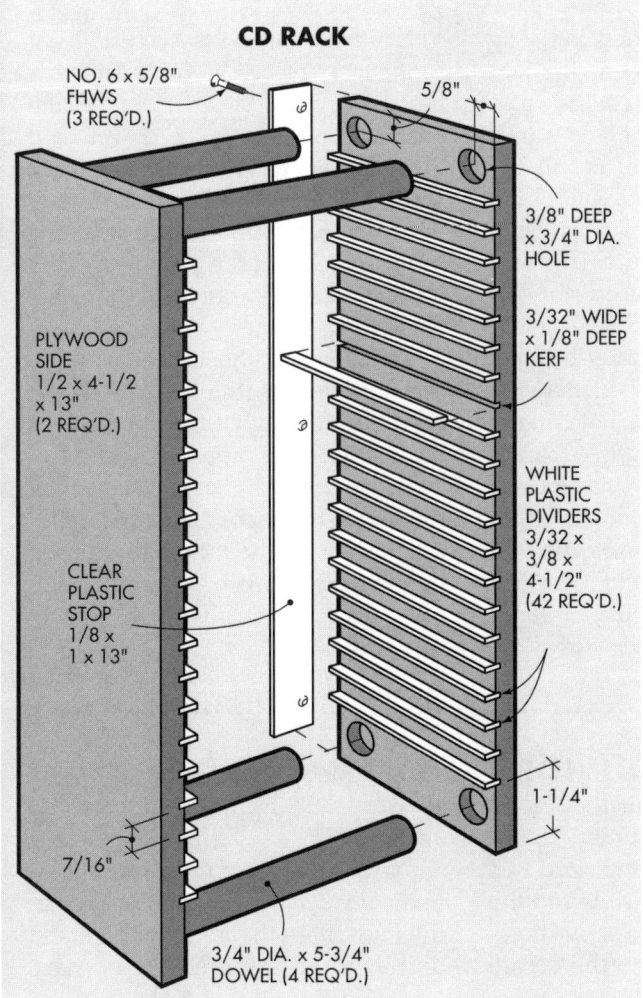

CD RACK

Labels on figure:
- NO. 6 x 5/8" FHWS (3 REQ'D.)
- 5/8"
- 3/8" DEEP x 3/4" DIA. HOLE
- 3/32" WIDE x 1/8" DEEP KERF
- PLYWOOD SIDE 1/2 x 4-1/2 x 13" (2 REQ'D.)
- WHITE PLASTIC DIVIDERS 3/32 x 3/8 x 4-1/2" (42 REQ'D.)
- CLEAR PLASTIC STOP 1/8 x 1 x 13"
- 7/16"
- 1-1/4"
- 3/4" DIA. x 5-3/4" DOWEL (4 REQ'D.)

Shown in Color on Page 3

To cut the plastic dividers, rip a long strip of plastic to width and then cut the pieces to length. Make more dividers than you'll need in case any get ruined. Because these pieces are small, use extra caution when cutting them. Be sure to use a stop block and blade guard.

Next, cut the sides to width. Make them a few inches longer than the finished size. The saw kerfs that hold the dividers in the sides are made with a series of repetitive cuts. You can make the cuts by moving the saw fence in 7/16-in. increments, but a better way is to use a jig made from a piece of 1/2-in. plywood that's screwed to a homemade sliding table for the table saw. First cut a 1/8-in.-deep kerf in the middle of the plywood. Then put the kerf side faceup and position the kerf 7/16 in. from the saw blade. Screw the plywood to the sliding table and then saw through the plywood.

To use the jig, lay a side on top of the jig and make the first cut about 1-1/2 in. from the end. Then put a 1/4-in.-wide scrap of the plastic

any or all of the parts from any material you have on hand: solid wood, plastic or metal.

Use a thin-kerf (3/32-in.) blade to cut the slots in the sides for the dividers. If you don't have a thin-kerf blade, use a standard-kerf (1/8-in.) blade and substitute 1/8-in. plastic. (In this case you'll need to increase the length of the sides to accommodate the wider slots.)

you're using for the dividers in the jig kerf. (The plastic will act as the kerf key.) Lay the side on top of the jig so the first cut and the kerf key lock together. Make a second cut in the side and then move the second cut over the kerf key. Repeat this step until you've made 21 cuts. This way you'll have perfectly spaced slots for the dividers.

Trim the ends of the sides 1-1/4 in. from the edge of the last kerf. Bore the 3/8-in.-deep x 3/4-in.-dia. holes in the sides for the support dowels. Accuracy is important, so align the drill bit carefully. Cut the support dowels to length and check the fit in the holes. Also cut the clear plastic stop and bore the holes and countersinks. Use a scraper to smooth the edges of the stop.

Sand all the parts with 150-grit sandpaper. It's best to paint the parts before you assemble them, but be sure to mask the ends of the dowels and dowel holes. Apply two coats of black spray enamel and sand lightly between coats with 320-grit stearated sandpaper. When the paint is dry, buff it with 0000 steel wool or an extra-fine Scotch-Brite pad.

To assemble the rack, first press the dividers into the kerfs. If the fit isn't snug enough to keep them in place, use a few drops of cyanoacrylate glue (Super Glue). Next, screw the stop to the back of one of the sides (the bottom, if the rack is to be used horizontally). Finally, glue the side assemblies together with the dowel supports.

2 SLIDE AND DIVIDE

The CD rack with the sliding divider (at right in the photo, opposite) is comprised of six pieces: two ends, a stretcher, two dowels and the sliding divider. Boring the dowel holes and cutting the notches for the 1x2 are the challenging tasks.

Start by laying out the pattern on the piece of 3/4-in. pine you've selected for one of the ends. Cut the shape with your sabre saw (or on a band saw, if you have one). Remove any saw marks with 80-grit sandpaper; then smooth the edges with 100-grit paper. Use the completed end piece as a template to lay out and mark the divider and the other end. For now, make believe the divider is an end piece — you'll cut it 1/4 in. shorter later. Cut and sand the end and divider.

Now lay out the notch and holes in the divider, which is still as large as the ends. Bore the holes with a hand drill or on a drill press if you have one. Use the divider to lay out the holes on the ends. These holes are only 3/8 in. deep and are best bored with a brad-point bit. If all you have is a spade bit, bore the holes only as deep as the spade bit allows without boring through. Before you move on, enlarge the holes in the divider slightly using a round rasp or file with coarse sandpaper wrapped around a smaller dowel. This helps the divider slide easily on the dowels

17
FURNITURE AND STORAGE PROJECTS

after the project has been assembled. Trim the divider to 5-7/8 in. tall; then lay out the notches on the divider and ends. Cut the notch in the divider with a sabre saw. The notch in the ends is only 3/8 in. deep and is cut most easily with a router and 3/4-in. straight bit. You can also

The "Tunes" box holds 38 CDs; the unit with the sliding divider holds about 40.

RACK WITH SLIDING DIVIDER

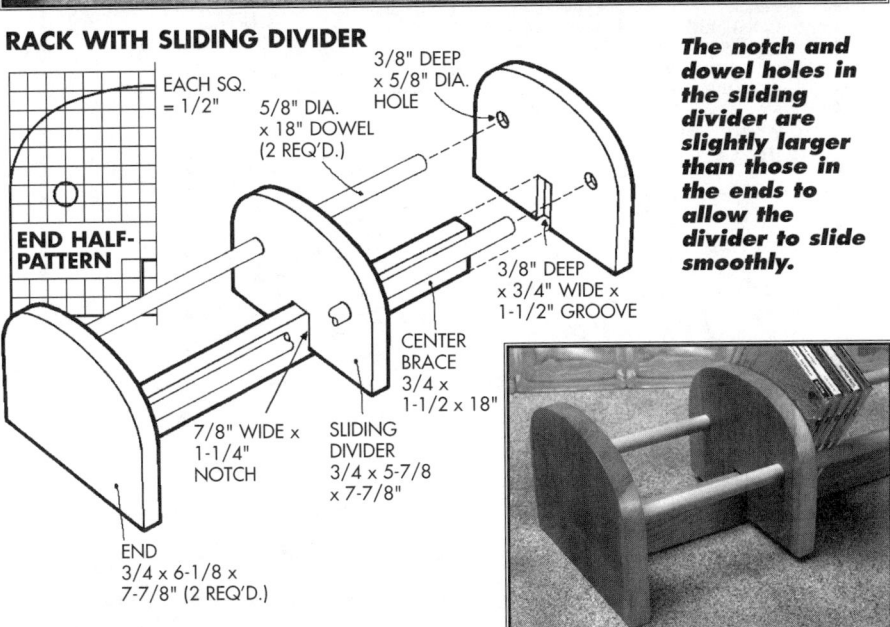

EACH SQ. = 1/2"
5/8" DIA. x 18" DOWEL (2 REQ'D.)
3/8" DEEP x 5/8" DIA. HOLE
END HALF-PATTERN
3/8" DEEP x 3/4" WIDE x 1-1/2" GROOVE
CENTER BRACE 3/4 x 1-1/2 x 18"
7/8" WIDE x 1-1/4" NOTCH
SLIDING DIVIDER 3/4 x 5-7/8 x 7-7/8"
END 3/4 x 6-1/8 x 7-7/8" (2 REQ'D.)

The notch and dowel holes in the sliding divider are slightly larger than those in the ends to allow the divider to slide smoothly.

cut the notches with a sharp 3/4-in.-wide chisel and mallet.

Cut the dowels and 1x2 stretcher (3/4 x 1-1/2 in. actual size) to length. Sand all parts with 150-grit sandpaper; then apply two coats of polyurethane to all the parts before assembling. To assemble the holder, glue the dowel and the 1x2 into one end and slide the divider on; then glue the dowels and 1x2 into the other end. Clamp until dry and the project is complete.

3 THE "TUNES" BOX

To build the "Tunes" box (see the photos on the opposite page and on p. 17) you need a sabre saw or circular saw. Use pine for all the parts. Cut parts wider than 5-1/2 in. from 1x8 pine (3/4 x 7-1/4 in. actual size), and use 1x6 pine (3/4 x 5-1/2 in. actual size) for the narrower parts. The pattern in the drawing shows how to cut a lid end and a base end or divider from a 3/4- x 5- x 6-in. piece.

Once you've cut all the parts to size, begin assembly by gluing and

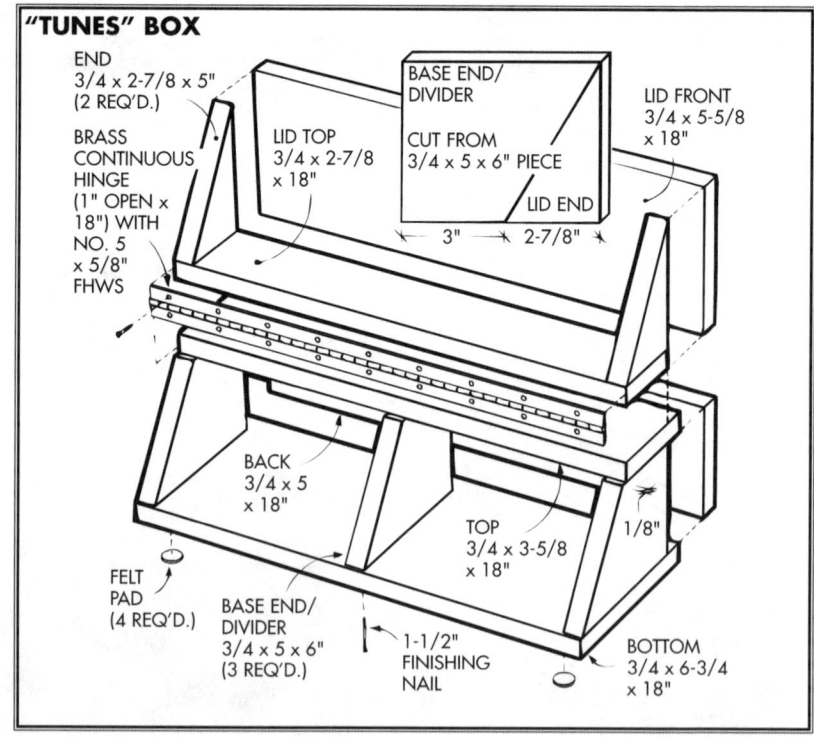

19
FURNITURE AND STORAGE PROJECTS

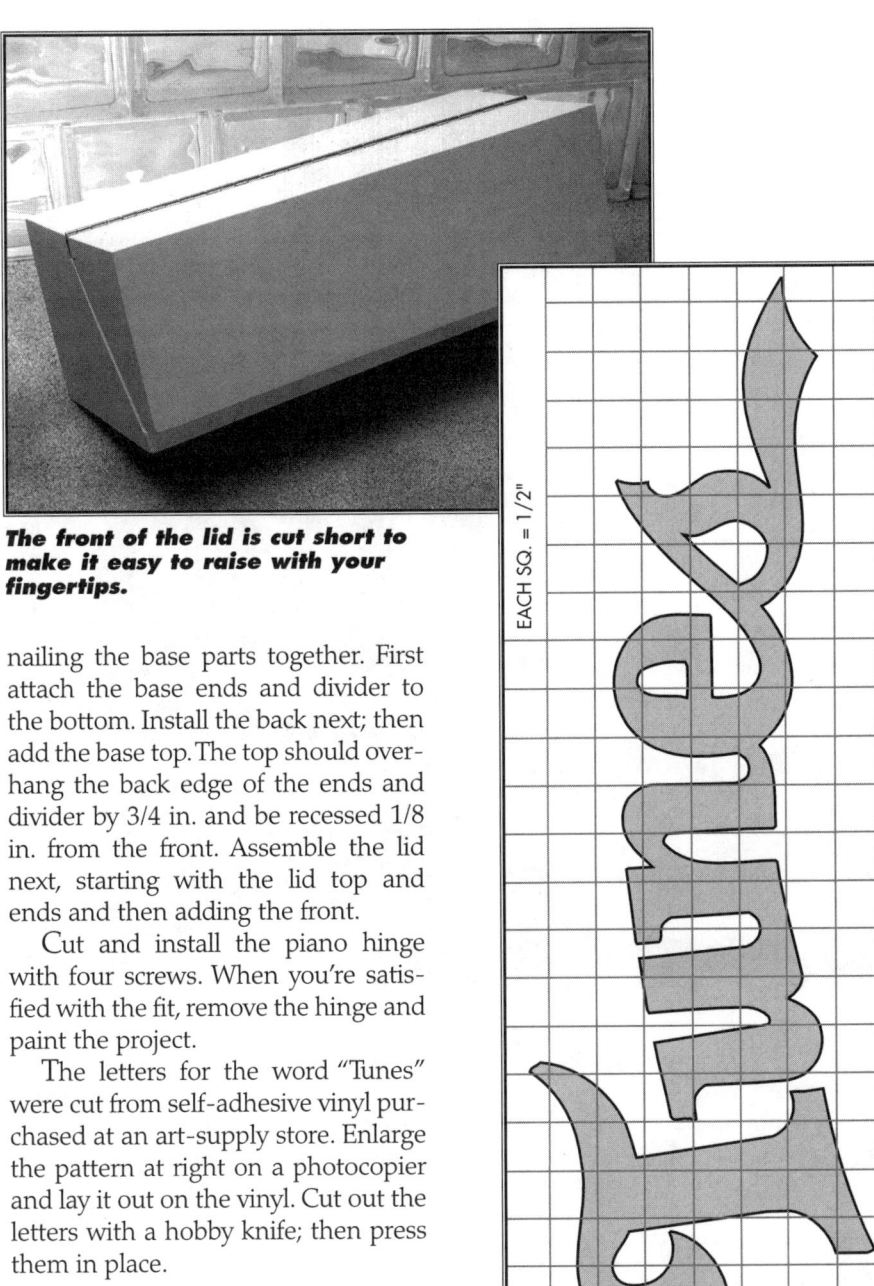

The front of the lid is cut short to make it easy to raise with your fingertips.

nailing the base parts together. First attach the base ends and divider to the bottom. Install the back next; then add the base top. The top should overhang the back edge of the ends and divider by 3/4 in. and be recessed 1/8 in. from the front. Assemble the lid next, starting with the lid top and ends and then adding the front.

Cut and install the piano hinge with four screws. When you're satisfied with the fit, remove the hinge and paint the project.

The letters for the word "Tunes" were cut from self-adhesive vinyl purchased at an art-supply store. Enlarge the pattern at right on a photocopier and lay it out on the vinyl. Cut out the letters with a hobby knife; then press them in place.

EACH SQ. = 1/2"

3 MAGAZINE RACKS

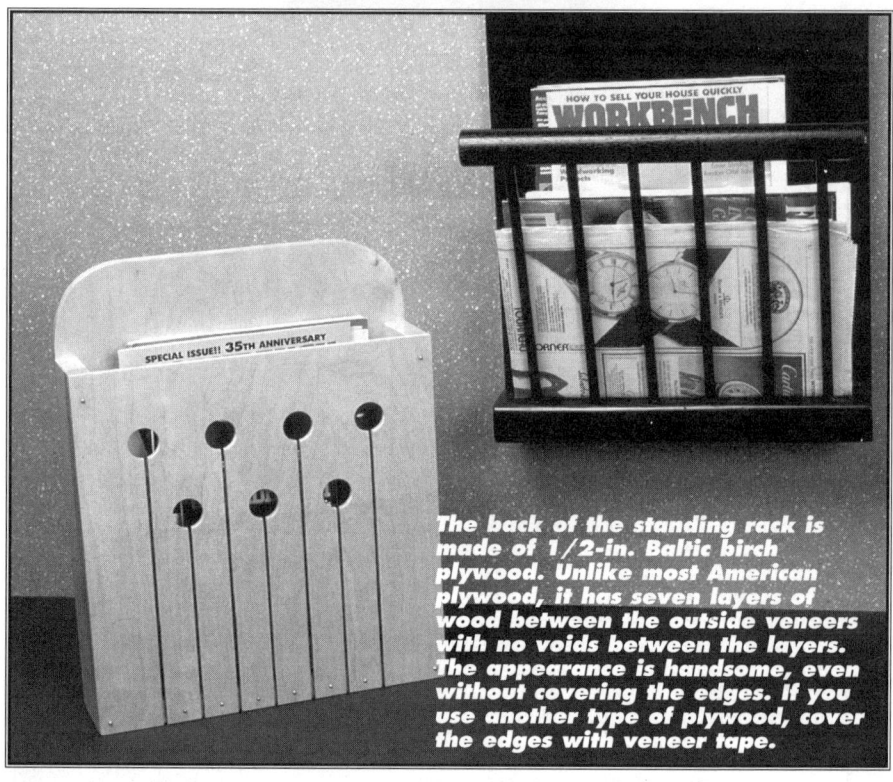

The back of the standing rack is made of 1/2-in. Baltic birch plywood. Unlike most American plywood, it has seven layers of wood between the outside veneers with no voids between the layers. The appearance is handsome, even without covering the edges. If you use another type of plywood, cover the edges with veneer tape.

ere are three ways to keep your favorite periodicals neat and easy to find. All can be customized to hold more magazines if necessary.

1 STANDING RACK

The standing plywood rack (at left in photo, above) is meant for a small space and holds a handful of periodicals. If you plan to apply a natural finish, as the rack shown has, use plywood that has at least one clear side. To start, cut the back to size; then use a sabre saw or scroll saw to shape the top corners. Next, cut the front to size. To make the decorative cutouts, mark the hole centers with an awl; then drill them with a 1-in. spade bit.

FURNITURE AND STORAGE PROJECTS

STANDING RACK

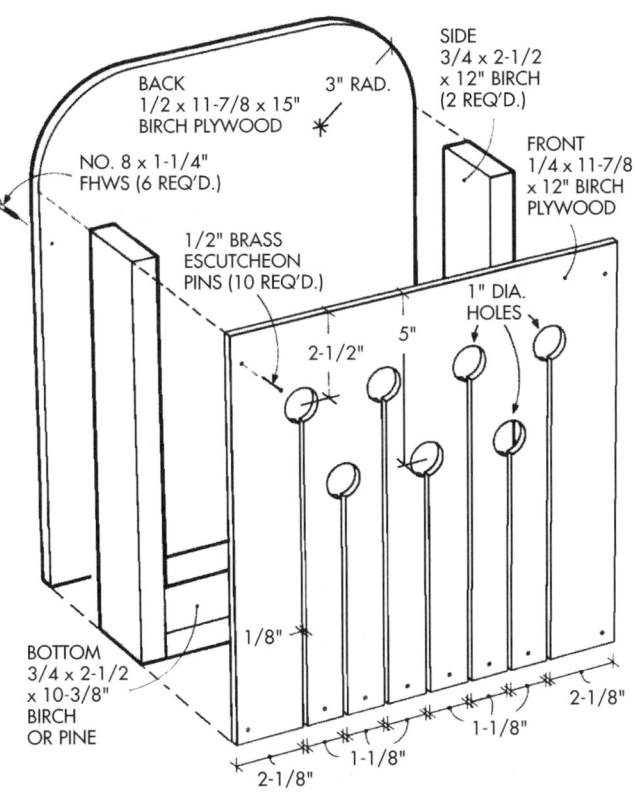

To prevent splintering on the back, clamp the front to a scrap piece of pine or plywood before you drill.

Now cut the sides and bottom. Glue and screw the back to the sides and bottom; then use brass escutcheon nails to attach the front. Two coats of satin polyurethane complete the project.

If you want to hang the rack on the wall, drill two hanging holes through the back to align with the decorative holes. This way you can use a screwdriver to drive the screws.

2 HANGING RACK

Because the hanging rack (at right in the photo, opposite) is painted, you can use plywood that has voids, but you'll need to fill the voids and sand before painting. For the bottom, rip 1 in. from a 2x4 to create a square edge to attach the back. Don't attach the bottom yet. Cut the 3/8-in.-dia. dowels to length; then mark the dowel holes on the bottom piece about 3/4 in. from the front edge, spaced as shown in the drawing on p. 22. To drill all of the holes at the same angle, cut a guide block. Draw a 20-degree angle on the face of a 3/4- x 2- x 2-in. block of wood. The angle doesn't have to be exact. (Use the Side Section view in the drawing as a guide; it's exactly 20 degrees.) Now cut along the line and your guide block is complete. Hold the block firmly on the magazine rack bottom and use it as a visual aid to maintain the drill bit at a 20-degree angle as you drill the six holes in the bottom.

Drilling the holes in the large dowel is also a bit tricky. Make sure to mark the holes first so they're spaced the same distance as the holes in the bottom. If you have a portable drill guide, use it to keep the drill boring straight into the dowel. (Clamp the dowel in a bench vise to keep it from moving.) If you have a drill press, place the dowel in a V-cradle, which you can cut from a 2x4 on a table saw. A V-cradle is made with two 45-degree cuts to form a vee that holds the dowel while you drill.

Attach the bottom to the back with glue and screws. Glue the dowels to the bottom; then glue the large dowel in place. Coat the entire project with a primer; then paint it. Use appropriate wall anchors and 2-in. screws to hang the rack.

HANGING RACK

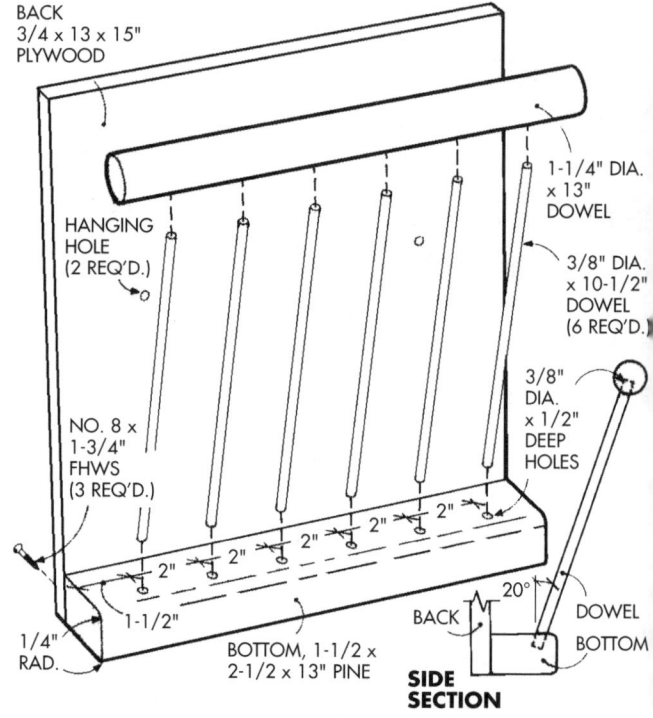

If you want the hanging rack with dowels to hold more magazines, make the bottom from a 2x6 instead of a 2x4. Attach the 2x6 with 2-1/4-in. flathead wood screws for extra strength.

• •

3 DISPLAY RACK

With a sabre saw, a drill and simple butt-joint construction, you can easily assemble an unobtrusive rack (photo, opposite) that keeps about three dozen magazines at your fingertips. You can adjust the height and width of the rack to suit the available wall space in your home or office.

Build the rack from straight 1x2 pine strips (3/4 x 1-1/2 in. actual size), or rip 1-1/2-in. strips from 3/4-in.-thick birch plywood. Cut all the pieces to length; then lay out the shelves and nail them to the sides. Attach the lips next with glue and nails.

FURNITURE AND STORAGE PROJECTS

DISPLAY RACK

The display rack holds about six magazines in each of its six pockets. To increase the storage capacity of the rack, make it taller or wider.

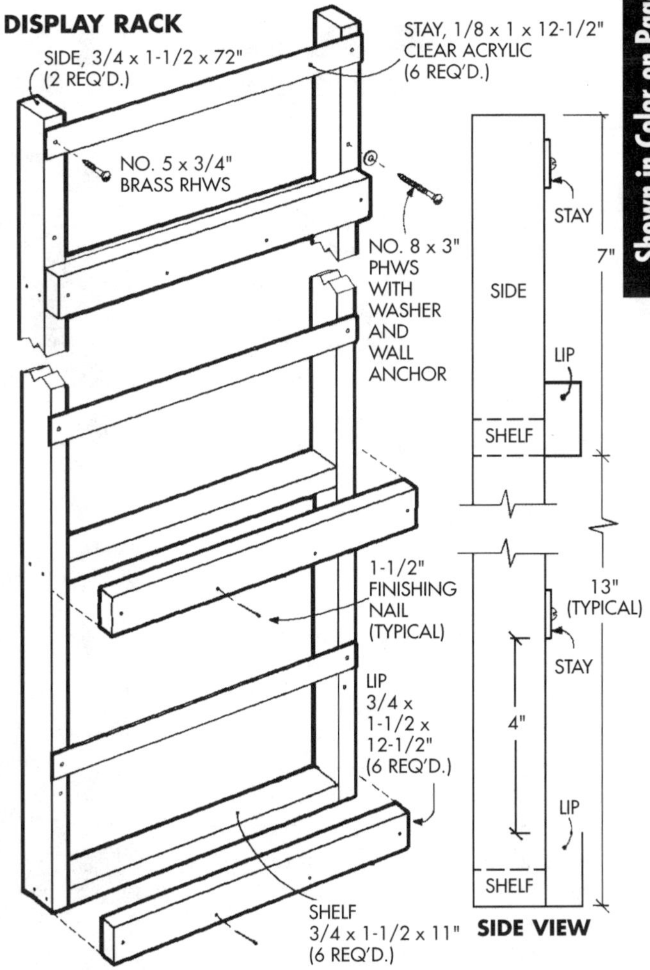

Set the nail heads below the surface and fill the cavities with wood putty or spackling compound. Sand the rack smooth and paint with a semigloss white paint.

Clear acrylic stays hold the magazines in place and keep them visible. Cut the stays from a 1/8- or 3/16-in.-thick sheet of acrylic using a table saw or a sabre saw with a plastic-cutting blade. Smooth the edges of the stays with sandpaper. Bore a clearance hole large enough for the screw shank to pass through in each end of the stays and screw them gently into place. (You can break the plastic if you drive in the screws too tight.)

To hang the rack, bore a clearance hole in each side as shown in the drawing above. Install wall anchors; then screw the rack in place.

COAT RACK

Quick & Easy

There's no need to clutter your closet with often-used coats and umbrellas when you can build an attractive rack that keeps them convenient.

The rack is made of plywood and 1-in.-dia. x 69-7/8-in.-long dowels. If you can't find dowels this long, you can splice two together at the middle ring. The 1-3/4-in.-dia. balls on the ends of the 1/2-in.-dia. dowel pegs can be purchased ready-made, or you can turn them on a lathe.

First, enlarge the ring patterns to full size on a photocopier, or draw them full size on graph paper. The base and the two lower rings are made from 3/4-in. plywood. You'll need to laminate two pieces of 1/2-in. plywood for the top ring. (It must be thicker to accommodate the 1/2-in.-dia. dowel pegs.) Trace the patterns on the plywood; then cut the circumferences with a band saw, sabre saw or scroll saw.

Use the patterns to mark the locations of the center cutouts and the holes for the dowels in all three rings. Note that the 1-in.-dia. holes in the two lower rings are through-holes, while the holes in the top ring are 7/8 in. deep. After you've bored the holes, cut out the centers with a scroll saw or sabre saw.

With a compass, draw a 16-in.-dia. circle for the base and cut it out; then center the bottom ring on the base and mark the locations of the through-holes for the dowels. Bore

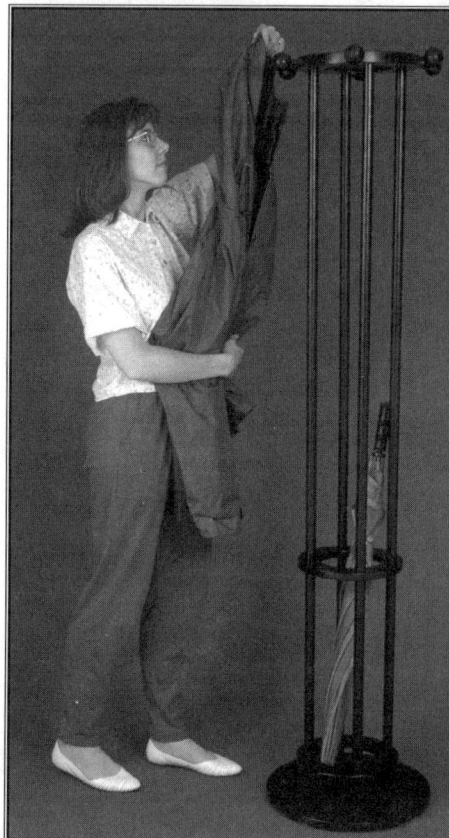

Corral jackets, umbrellas and hats with a contemporary variation of the traditional coat tree.

the holes; then cut the 1/4-in. x 11-in.-dia. plywood bottom (see drawing, Side View) and attach it with glue and 3/4-in. brads.

To assemble the rack, first slip on the two lower rings, but don't glue them yet. Glue the dowels to the base; then apply glue to each dowel where

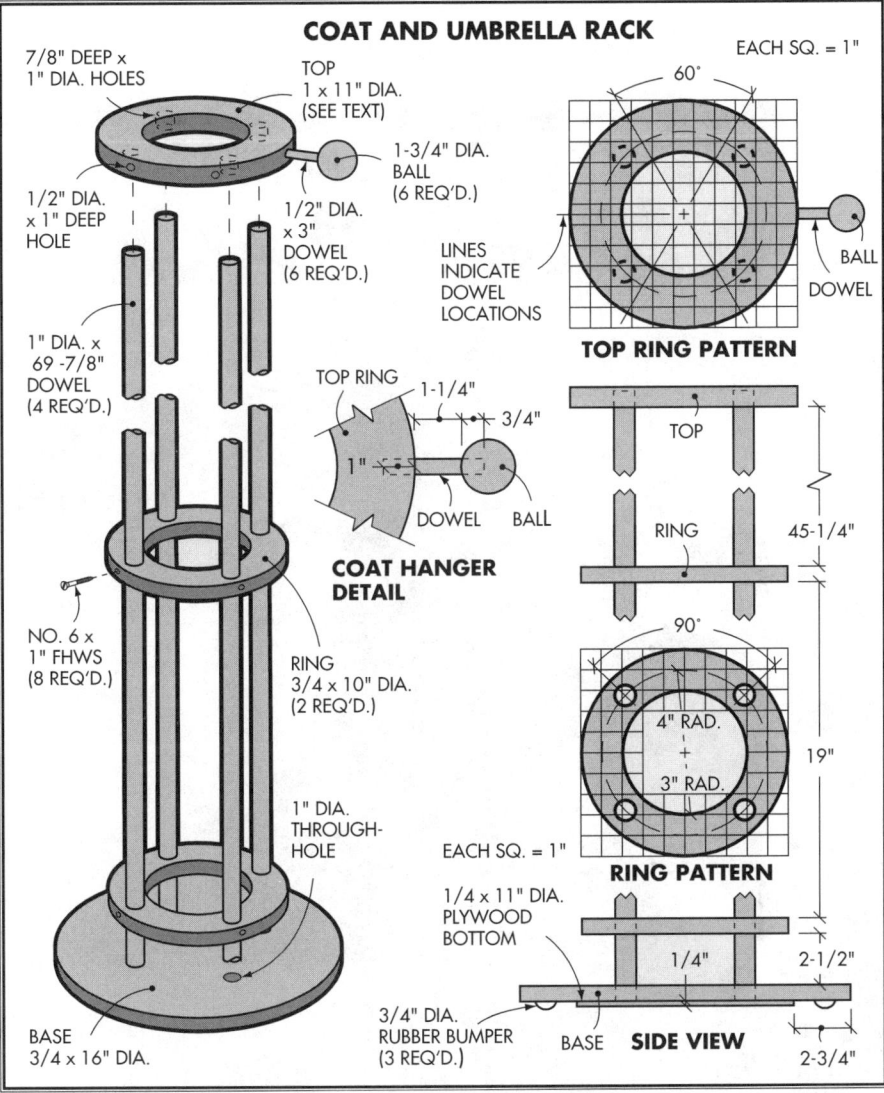

the rings will be and slide them into position. Put clamps on the dowels just under the rings to hold them in place; then bore pilot holes and countersinks for the no. 6 x 1-in. screws. Drive the screws; then sand all edges and fill the holes with wood putty.

Before you attach the top ring, assemble the pegs and glue them in place. The top ring is simply glued onto the dowels. Finally, brush on a primer and sand; then apply two coats of spray enamel, sanding lightly between coats with 320-grit stearated paper. When the paint is dry, attach the three rubber bumpers to the bottom of the base.

FISHERMAN'S WADER RACK

Hang by your heels — or at least hang fishermen's waders by their heels — in this wall-mounted rack. Attach the rack to wooden studs with screws or to drywall or plaster with hollow-wall fasteners.

Surprise your favorite fisherman with a storage rack for his waders. Hanging waders keeps them from folding over, which can cause leaks. You don't have to be a fisherman to appreciate this gift; the rack is an ideal place to store insulated snow boots.

FURNITURE AND STORAGE PROJECTS

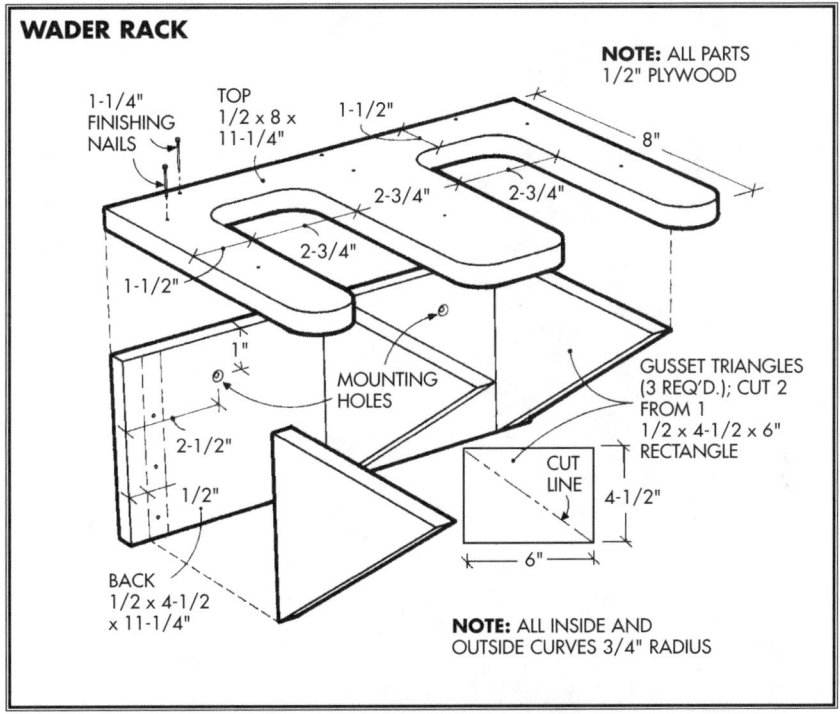

The rack is made from Baltic birch plywood, but any 1/2-in.-thick plywood will work. Although a band saw, scroll saw or sabre saw makes cutting the parts easy, you can use a coping saw and still do a good job. You'll also need 120-grit sandpaper, glue, 1-1/4-in. finishing nails and a can of spray paint (any color, any type) for finishing the rack.

Cut all the parts to size. Note that the easiest way to make the triangular gussets is to cut two of them from one rectangular piece (see drawing). Next, draw the slots for the boots on the top with a pencil. All the inside and outside curves are 3/4 in. radius. Cut the slots carefully and then sand all the rough edges smooth.

If any of the pieces have voids or imperfections on the edges, fill them with wood putty. After the putty is dry, sand all the surfaces smooth and round over all sharp edges.

Attach the gussets to the back with glue and nails (use an air nailer if you have one); then glue and nail the top in place. Set all the nail heads slightly below the surface and fill with wood putty. Do a final sanding before painting.

For the smoothest finish, spray on four or five light coats and scuff-sand between coats. Make the last coat a little heavier so the paint has a chance to flow out flat.

Quick & Easy

COFFEE MUG TREE

Combining hardwoods turns an everyday accessory into a handsome gift. The tree has six pegs, which you can turn on a lathe or purchase ready-made.

Keep mugs handy and on display with a tree made from contrasting woods. The mug tree shown in the photo is made from walnut and oak, but you could use mahogany and maple, cherry and birch or any other combination of woods you like.

You can buy mug-tree pegs or turn your own using the pattern in the drawing. Most store-bought pegs are made of birch or oak. However, you might want to substitute traditional pegs or classic Shaker pegs, which are available in birch, oak, walnut, maple and cherry.

Begin by planing the walnut to 1/8- and 1/4-in.-thick pieces for the trunk (see drawing). If you don't have

FURNITURE AND STORAGE PROJECTS

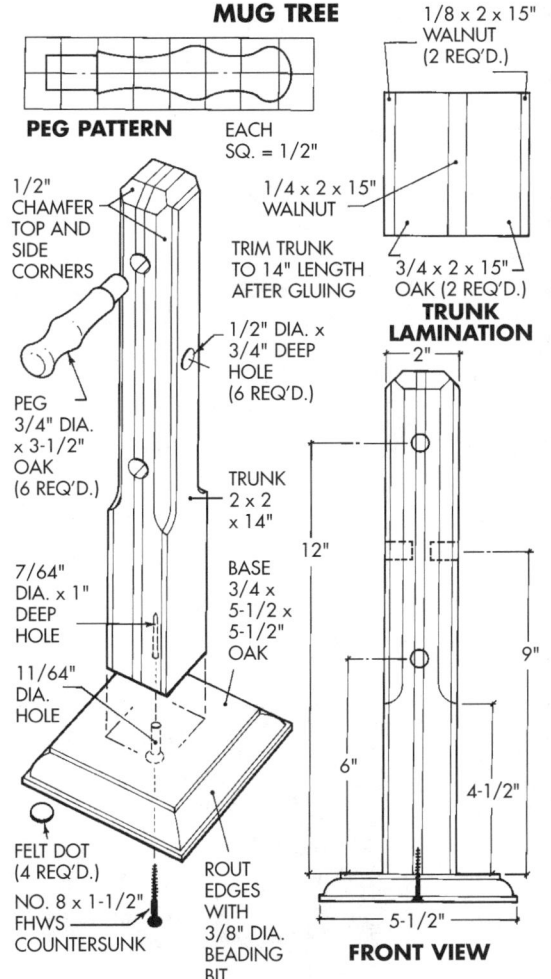

MUG TREE

PEG PATTERN — EACH SQ. = 1/2"

1/2" CHAMFER TOP AND SIDE CORNERS

PEG 3/4" DIA. x 3-1/2" OAK (6 REQ'D.)

7/64" DIA. x 1" DEEP HOLE

11/64" DIA. HOLE

FELT DOT (4 REQ'D.)

NO. 8 x 1-1/2" FHWS COUNTERSUNK

1/8 x 2 x 15" WALNUT (2 REQ'D.)

1/4 x 2 x 15" WALNUT

TRIM TRUNK TO 14" LENGTH AFTER GLUING

3/4 x 2 x 15" OAK (2 REQ'D.)

TRUNK LAMINATION

1/2" DIA. x 3/4" DEEP HOLE (6 REQ'D.)

TRUNK 2 x 2 x 14"

BASE 3/4 x 5-1/2 x 5-1/2" OAK

ROUT EDGES WITH 3/8" DIA. BEADING BIT

FRONT VIEW — 2", 12", 9", 6", 4-1/2", 5-1/2"

1 Rip stock to 2 in. wide on a band saw or table saw. Don't worry about saw marks — you'll sand or scrape them off after you glue the trunk together.

2 Let the glue set for a few minutes before clamping so the laminations won't slide apart. Don't overtighten the clamps.

Shown in Color on Page 4

a planer, resaw the stock with your table saw or band saw and sand out the saw marks. Also, cut the 3/4-in.-thick oak trunk pieces. Rip all pieces to a 2-in. width (photo 1). Crosscut the pieces to about 15 in. — you'll trim them to the final 14-in. length after you glue them together.

Arrange the workpieces on a work surface as follows: 1/8-in. walnut, 3/4- in. oak, 1/4-in. walnut, 3/4-in. oak and 1/8-in. walnut. Use a paintbrush, roller or trowel to apply an even coat of glue to all the mating surfaces. Let the pieces sit for a minute or two so the wood has a chance to absorb the glue.

Stack the pieces in the order you arranged them, and clamp the strips with at least three bar clamps or C-clamps (photo 2). If your clamps don't have protective jaw pads, it's a good idea to use wood blocks between the clamp jaws and the stock to prevent denting and scratching. Wipe away glue seepage with a damp sponge, and let the assembly stand for several hours or overnight.

Trim about 1/2 in. from one end of the trunk in a miter box with a backsaw or on a stationary power saw. Then cut the opposite end so both ends are square.

Use a stationary or portable belt sander and medium-grit belt to sand the glued surfaces of the trunk to a smooth, even finish. (Make sure you remove all saw-blade marks.)

Trim 1x6 oak scrap to 5-1/2 in. sq. for the tree base. Sand the edges of the end grain smooth with a belt sander and 120-grit belt.

Using a pencil and straightedge, find the center of the bottom by drawing diagonal lines across the bottom from corner to corner. At the intersection of the lines, centerpunch a drill starter hole (photo 3). Do likewise on the bottom.

Drill an 11/64-in.-dia. hole through the base center and countersink it for a no. 8 x 1-1/2-in. flathead wood screw. Then drill a 7/64-in.-dia. x 1-in.-deep pilot hole in the bottom of the trunk.

Use a combination square to draw lines across the trunk to indicate peg positions (see drawing). Now set the square for 1 in. and make a mark across each line (photo 4). Centerpunch a starter hole and drill a 1/2-in.-dia. x 3/4-in.-deep hole at each spot. A drill press works best for this

3 Mark diagonal lines on the trunk bottom and base. Use a centerpunch before boring the hole so the drill bit won't skate off center.

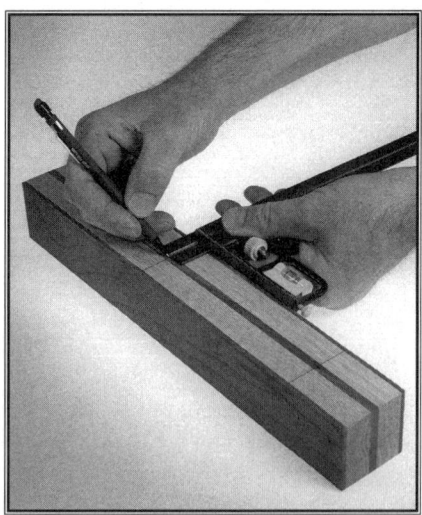

4 To find peg hole centers, set the combination square to 1 in. and make a mark. Check the opposite side to see if the mark is centered.

FURNITURE AND STORAGE PROJECTS

job, but a hand drill is fine provided you take care to drill the holes perpendicular to the stock.

With a router mounted in a router table, set a 1/2-in. chamfering bit for about a 1/4-in. depth of cut; then chamfer the long corner edges and top edges of the trunk (photo 5). Reset the bit for a 1/2-in. depth of cut and repeat the process. (Note: Chamfer the full length of the trunk, or start the chamfer about 4-1/2 in. from the bottom, as shown.) Next, rout the edges of the base on the router table with a 3/8-in. beading bit or any other suitable bit, such as a 1/2-in. rounding over bit or Roman ogee bit.

Sand the base and trunk with a pad sander and 120- and 220-grit sandpaper. Slightly round over the sharp edges of the base as you proceed (just enough to soften the appearance). Then clean the pieces thoroughly with a tack cloth and attach the base to the trunk with glue and a no. 8 x 1-1/2-in. flathead wood screw.

Carefully squeeze a small amount of wood glue into a peg hole and turn a peg into the hole to firmly seat it. Install the remaining pegs the same way and let the tree stand for at least two hours.

Clean the tree to remove dust and finish it. The tree shown was finished with Danish oil. Apply according to the manufacturer's directions and let stand for 24 hours. Apply a coat of wax and let stand 10 minutes; then buff with a clean, soft rag. Finally, attach a self-adhesive felt dot at each corner of the bottom of the base.

5 *Use a router table to chamfer the trunk corners. Make two passes, increasing the depth of cut on the second pass. If you hold the router by hand, clamp the workpiece securely in a bench vise.*

32 Quick & Easy

KNIFE BLOCK WITH CUTTING BOARD

The block keeps knives safely sheathed and has storage for a cutting board.

his knife block has built-in storage for a cutting board, eliminating the temptation to work without one. The storage area even has drying space so you can put the cutting board away right after washing it.

Make the project out of a tight-grained hard wood such as maple to prevent bacteria from colonizing in the pores. Begin by edge-gluing 32-in.-long strips of 1-1/2-in.-wide maple to make a single 7-1/2- x 32-in.

FURNITURE AND STORAGE PROJECTS

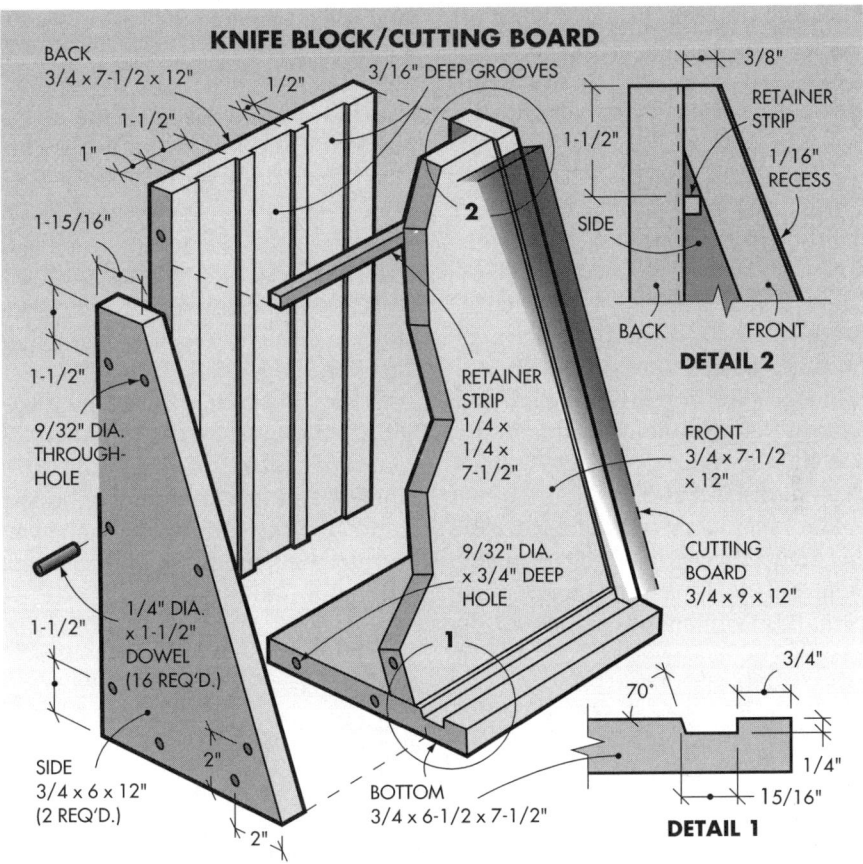

piece. After the glue dries, plane or sand the piece until it is smooth; then cut the front, back and bottom. The front is angled 70 degrees, so set your table saw at 20 degrees to cut the top and bottom edges.

Using a table saw or router, cut the grooves for the knives in the back. If you use a table saw, make repeated passes with a rip blade, or use a dado set if you have one. Three 1-1/2-in.-wide grooves are shown in the drawing, but you can change the number of grooves and their width to fit the knives you use.

Cut a 1/4-in.-deep groove in the bottom to hold the cutting board (see drawing, Detail 1). Note that the back of the groove is sloped 70 degrees. Use a table saw to cut the angles on the top of the front as shown in Detail 2.

Cut the sides from solid stock, if possible, or edge-glue narrower stock to get a piece 6 in. wide x 20 in. long. (By flipping the pattern, you can get both sides from a 20-in.-long board.)

Bore 9/32-in.-dia. through-holes in the sides as shown in the drawing. Locate the holes 3/8 in. from the edges. Glue the retainer strip to the back (Detail 2).

Assemble the pieces without glue (two-sided tape will help hold them together temporarily) and clamp. Note that the front is recessed 1/16 in. When you're satisfied with the fit, insert a 9/32-in.-dia. drill bit through the holes in the sides and bore 3/4-in.-deep holes in the front, back and bottom. Remove the clamps and any tape you may have used. Cut 16 dowels and lay them aside.

The knife block is assembled with glue and dowels. Apply glue to the joints and the dowels as you assemble them. (Use white glue; it dries slowly and will give you time to assemble the parts.) Begin by attaching one side to the front and back. Drive in the dowels with a wood mallet. If the end of the dowel isn't flush with the side, don't force it — you can cut it flush later. Next, attach the bottom to the side. Turn the block on its side and add the other side; then clamp.

Remove any dried glue and cut the dowels flush with the sides; then break the edges with sandpaper.

Make the cutting board by edge-gluing 3/4-in.-thick strips. After the glue dries, plane or sand both sides until the board is smooth. You can apply two coats of polyurethane varnish to the knife block, but leave the cutting board unfinished.

FURNITURE AND STORAGE PROJECTS

NECKLACE HANGER

This simple holder keeps necklaces and bracelets separated and allows them to hang, preventing kinks.

You'll need a piece of 5/8- x 6- x 12-in. stock (the rack shown in the photo is made of sycamore), a serrated picture hanger and seven small drawer pulls with integral wood screws. The rosette and drawer-pull base plate are optional.

Begin by enlarging the pattern to full size using a photocopier, or draw the pattern on graph paper. Trace around the pattern onto the stock and mark the holes for the drawer pulls. Using a band saw, scroll saw or sabre saw, cut along the traced line. Remove the saw marks from the stock with a half-round smooth file; then sand the edges smooth and ease the corners.

This easy-to-make necklace hanger keeps jewelry from becoming tangled.

The knobs shown had screw threads that required 1/8-in.-dia. x 1/2-in.-deep pilot holes. Buy your knobs and bore test holes of different sizes in scrap wood before you drill into the workpiece. Sand the piece lightly and finish with Danish oil or varnish. Finally, screw in the knobs and attach the picture hanger to the back about 1 in. from the top.

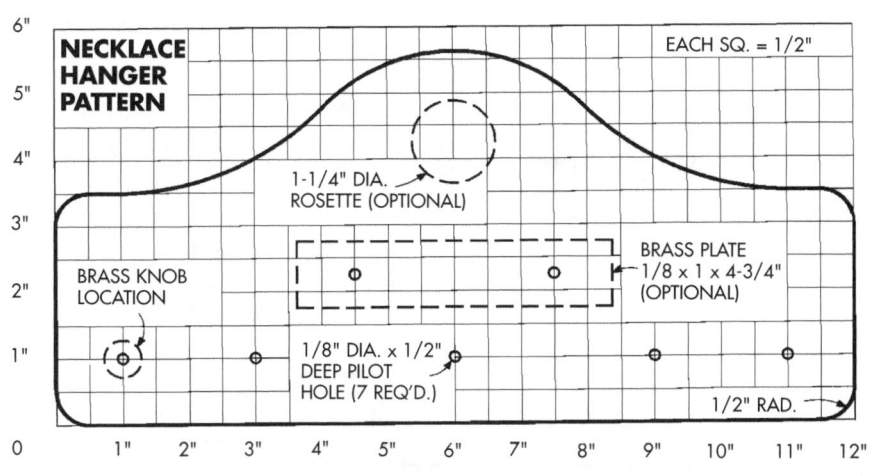

TIE RACK

This tie rack is a simple project you can complete in one evening.

Anyone who wears ties to the office can use a closet-mounted tie rack. The rack is made of maple with birch dowels and finished with a rich, wipe-on fruitwood oil finish. Construction is straightforward, and assembly is easy.

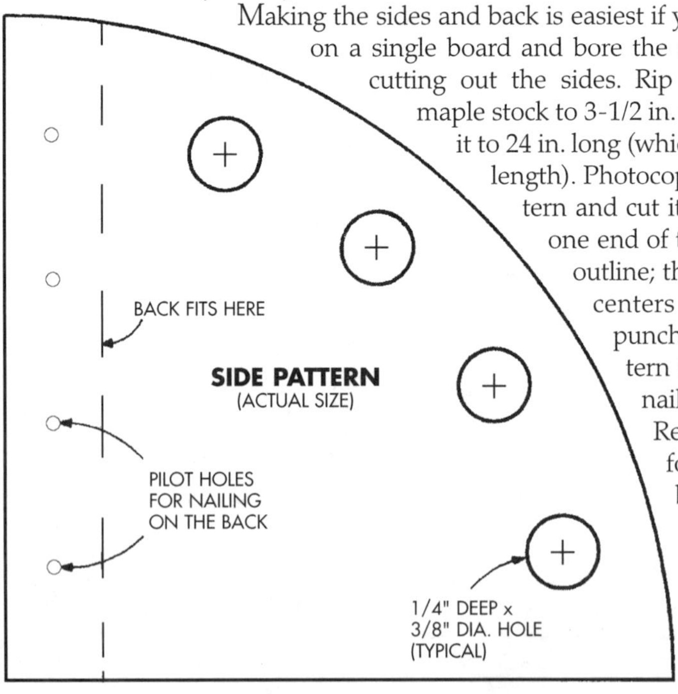

Making the sides and back is easiest if you lay them all out on a single board and bore the dowel holes before cutting out the sides. Rip a piece of 1/2-in. maple stock to 3-1/2 in. wide; then crosscut it to 24 in. long (which adds a little extra length). Photocopy the full-size pattern and cut it out; then lay it on one end of the board. Trace the outline; then mark the dowel centers with an awl or punch through the pattern (photo 1). Mark the nail positions as well. Repeat this procedure for the second side by flipping the pattern upside down. This will create sides that are mirror images.

Bore 1/4-in.-deep

SIDE PATTERN
(ACTUAL SIZE)

BACK FITS HERE

PILOT HOLES FOR NAILING ON THE BACK

1/4" DEEP x 3/8" DIA. HOLE (TYPICAL)

x 3/8-in.-dia. dowel holes with a brad-point bit. Use a stop collar or wrap a piece of tape around your drill bit so you don't bore too deep. Next, bore pilot holes for the nails with a brad chucked in a drill (photo 2). Also bore the countersink and clearance holes in the back for the mounting screws.

Cut the curved part of the sides with a band saw or scroll saw (if you're limited to hand tools, a coping saw or sabre saw work fine); then cut the sides from the board. Remove the saw marks from the edges of the sides by clamping both pieces together and smoothing them with a belt sander (photo 3, p. 38). You can also use a rasp or 80-grit sandpaper wrapped around a block of wood to do the final shaping. Sand the curved sides into a smooth arc — they don't have to exactly match the pattern — then sand smooth with 120-grit sandpaper. Cut the back and dowels to length; then sand all parts smooth, easing the edges slightly.

To assemble the tie rack, glue and nail one side to the back with 1-1/4-in. finishing nails. Apply a drop of glue to one end of each of the dowels and insert them into the glued-up side. Put glue in the dowel holes on the second side; then glue and nail it to the back (photo 4). Remove glue squeeze-out with a damp cloth.

1 Align the template with the bottom of the board. Mark the dowel and nail locations.

2 Use a finishing nail with the head cut off as a drill bit to make pilot holes for the nails in the back edge of the sides.

Shown in Color on Page 4

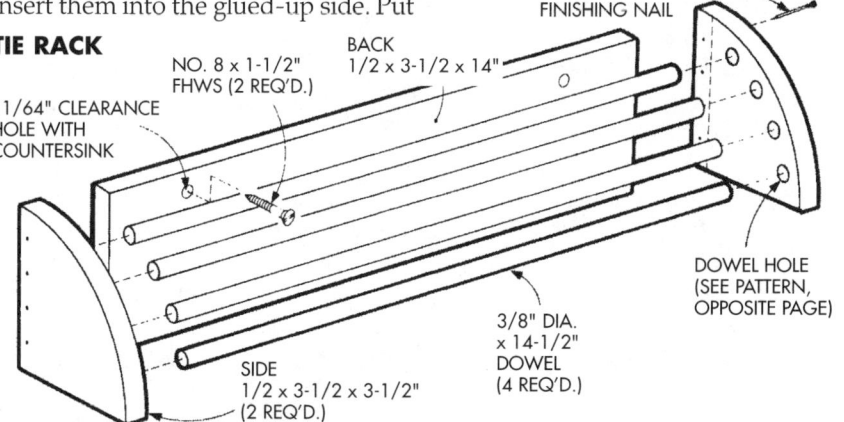

TIE RACK

- 1-1/4" FINISHING NAIL
- BACK 1/2 x 3-1/2 x 14"
- NO. 8 x 1-1/2" FHWS (2 REQ'D.)
- 11/64" CLEARANCE HOLE WITH COUNTERSINK
- SIDE 1/2 x 3-1/2 x 3-1/2" (2 REQ'D.)
- 3/8" DIA. x 14-1/2" DOWEL (4 REQ'D.)
- DOWEL HOLE (SEE PATTERN, OPPOSITE PAGE)

SHELVES TO GO

3 Clamp the ends together so you can shape them into a matched pair. A belt sander makes it easy.

4 Glue and nail the sides to the back with 1-1/4-in. finishing nails. Set all nail heads with a nail set; then fill the holes with wood putty.

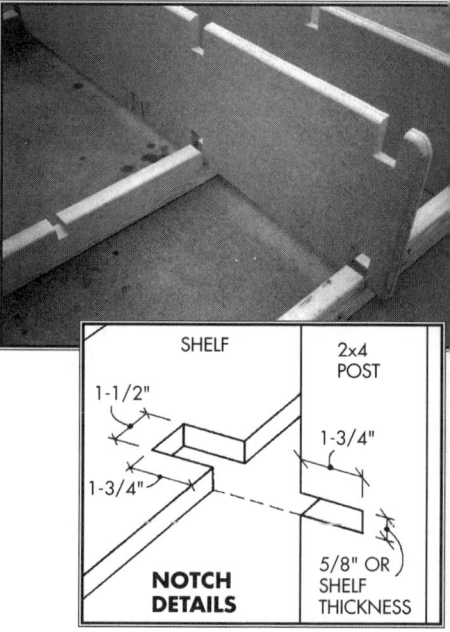

NOTCH DETAILS

When the glue hardens, set the nails below the surface and fill with wood putty. When dry, sand smooth; then remove sawdust with a tack rag.

Apply a generous coating of Danish oil to finish the rack. Allow the oil to penetrate into the wood for five minutes or so; then wipe off the excess. Repeat the process until the maple has absorbed as much finish as possible; then buff away the excess. Allow the rack to dry overnight; then polish with wax for more luster.

The rack should be installed with two flathead wood screws driven into suitable wall anchors.

These shelves are sturdy enough for books, tools or toys, and they're inexpensive to make and easy to disassemble for transportation. They can be built from scrap 2x4s and plywood or particleboard. A 4x8 sheet of plywood or particleboard will make five 9-1/2-in.-wide or four 11-7/8-in.-wide shelves. The unit shown in the photo, opposite, uses less than one sheet of 5/8-in.-thick particleboard and some 2x4s.

39
FURNITURE AND STORAGE PROJECTS

Notching is the key to the shelves' strength, portability and easy construction. The assembled unit is 3-1/2 ft. tall x 6 ft. long. Toys dictate the spacing between the shelves.

SHELVES TO GO

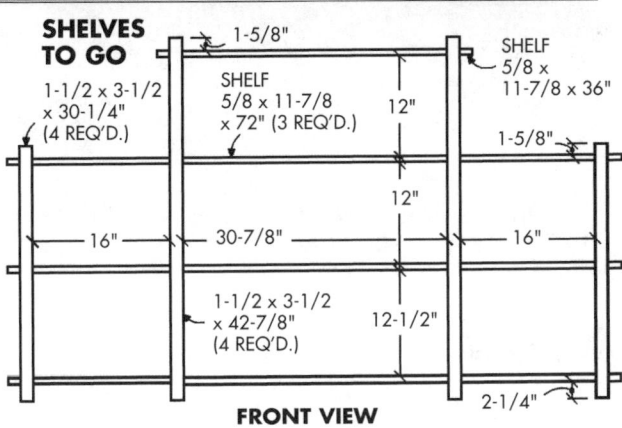

FRONT VIEW

Use a sabre saw to cut the notches. The notches do not have to be too snug. Don't risk splitting or breaking the wood by cutting the notches too close to the end of a 2x4 or a particleboard shelf. Leave a minimum of a couple of inches. (The unit shown had to fit beneath a window and hold toys of a specific size, so the notches in the 2x4s were cut closer to the ends of the boards than is recommended.)

To assemble a unit, lay the rear 2x4s on edge with the notches faceup. Insert the bottom shelf into each 2x4 and so forth for the remaining shelves. Then place the front 2x4s on the shelves and gently tap them into place with a hammer and a protective block. The unit is light enough for one person to pivot it into place.

NEWSPAPER RECYCLING BIN

This bin holds a stack of newspapers and keeps twine handy for tying up bundles ready for recycling.

epending on your reading habits, this bin keeps weeks or months of newspapers neatly stored until you're ready to recycle. You can make it from any kind of lumber or plywood.

The bin pictured has 1/2-in. birch plywood sides and 3/4-in. birch plywood slats. Start by cutting the slats to the sizes shown in the drawing. If you're working on a table saw, radial arm saw or power miter box, use a stop block when crosscutting the slats to ensure all like pieces are the same length. Once they are exact, glue the ends of the short slats and clamp them. You can also cut the slats with a miter box and backsaw. Clamp the box to a sturdy worktable and clamp a stop block outside of the miter box. Move the stop block for each of the three slat lengths.

When the back and bottom frames are assembled, glue and clamp them together. The bin was assembled with

FURNITURE AND STORAGE PROJECTS

NEWSPAPER RECYCLING BIN

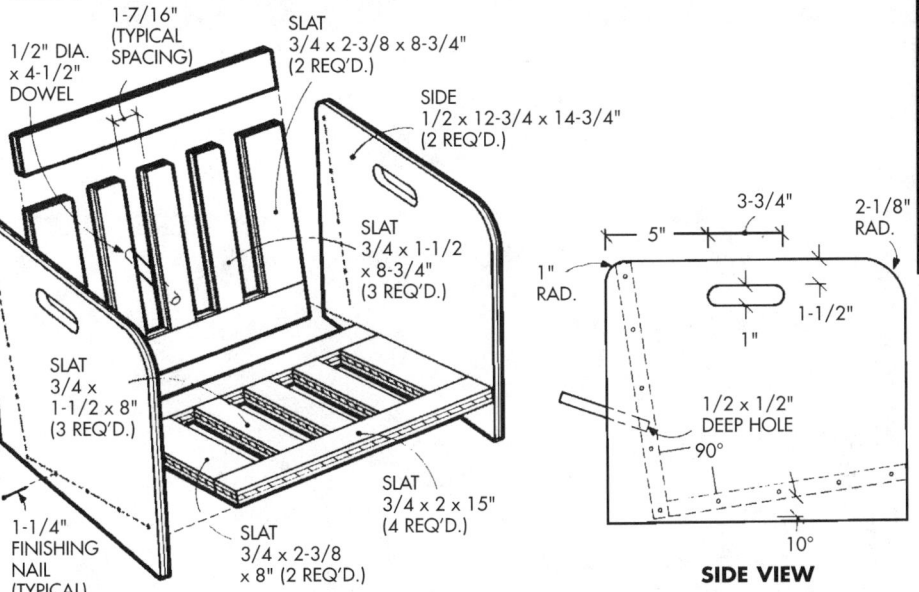

SIDE VIEW

1-1/4-in. finishing nails and glue. You might prefer to use 1/4-in.-dia. dowels to align the assembly and then drive nails or screws. The frames should be perpendicular to each other (although the angle doesn't have to be exact — it's OK if it is slightly off).

Cut the sides from 1/4- to 3/4-in. plywood. Relieve the sharp edges with sandpaper; then lay out the handholds and curved corners. The curves on the bin shown were laid out using a one-quart paint can for the front and a quarter on the back. Cut the curves with a sabre saw, band saw or scroll saw. Bore the ends of the handholds with a 1-in.-dia. drill bit; then complete the cutout with a sabre saw or a scroll saw. Relieve the edges with sandpaper. (You may want to use a rat-tail file on the handholds.)

Lay one side with the inside face-up on a worktable and place the assembled L-shape frame on top. Angle it as shown in the drawing. Now lay the second side on top of the frame. Check that the second side is in the same relative position to the frame as the side lying on the table; then make a pencil mark to outline the frame position on both sides. Lightly glue the edges of the frame; then clamp the parts together. Use finishing nails to strengthen the assembly. (The length of the nails depends on the thickness of the sides.) Set the nail heads and fill the holes with wood putty. Add a coat of polyurethane and the project is almost complete.

Finally, insert a dowel in the back to hold a ball of twine for binding the newspapers. Angle the dowel up so the twine will stay put.

Quick & Easy

KNOCK-DOWN TABLE

ABOVE: This table won't take up much space in a moving van — it's designed to be easily disassembled for convenient transportation.

RIGHT: After the edge-banding and ends have been attached, the table consists of three parts: the top and two legs. A 1/4- x 12- x 17-1/16-in. piece of glass (not shown) fits between the ends.

Convenience is the idea behind this simple design. Although it makes a sturdy end table or nightstand, you can disassemble it for compact storage by removing four screws.

The table is made of 3/4-in. birch plywood with poplar edge-banding to cover the plywood edges. Begin by cutting all pieces to size. Cut the legs, top and edge-banding slightly longer than the dimensions in the drawing; you'll cut them to the exact length after

FURNITURE AND STORAGE PROJECTS

you've attached the edge-banding.
Fasten the edge-banding to the legs and top with yellow glue and 1-1/4-in. finishing nails. When the glue is dry, smooth the joints with a sanding block and cut the 45-degree bevels on the tops and bottoms of the legs with a table saw. Sand the bevels smooth.

Lay out the notches so they are vertically centered on the legs and cut them on a table saw with a dado blade or with a router. Square the bottom of the notches with a sharp chisel; then sand the cut edges smooth. Assemble the legs to check the fit of the notches — they should fit together easily. If you have to use force to fit the legs together, the notches need to be enlarged. Keep in mind that the paint will make the fit tighter; you want to be able to take the legs apart without scratching the paint.

Cut the top to its exact length and attach the ends with glue and finishing nails. Assemble the legs and top and mark the locations for the no. 6 x 1-1/4-in. flathead wood screws (refer to drawing). Bore shank holes and countersinks in the top and pilot holes in the legs, but don't drive in the four screws until after you've painted the pieces.

Fill all nail holes with wood putty and sand all the pieces smooth. Apply an oil-base (alkyd) primer to all surfaces; then finish with an oil-base enamel. When the paint is dry, reassemble the table and drive the four flathead wood screws through the top.

The glass should be the same width as the top but 1/16 in. shorter than the length so it will fit between the ends. Set the glass in place and mark the location of the screws on the glass; then attach round self-adhesive foam cushions (available at hardware stores) to the underside of the glass. The cushions will cover up the screws and keep the glass from sliding.

Shown in Color on Page 5

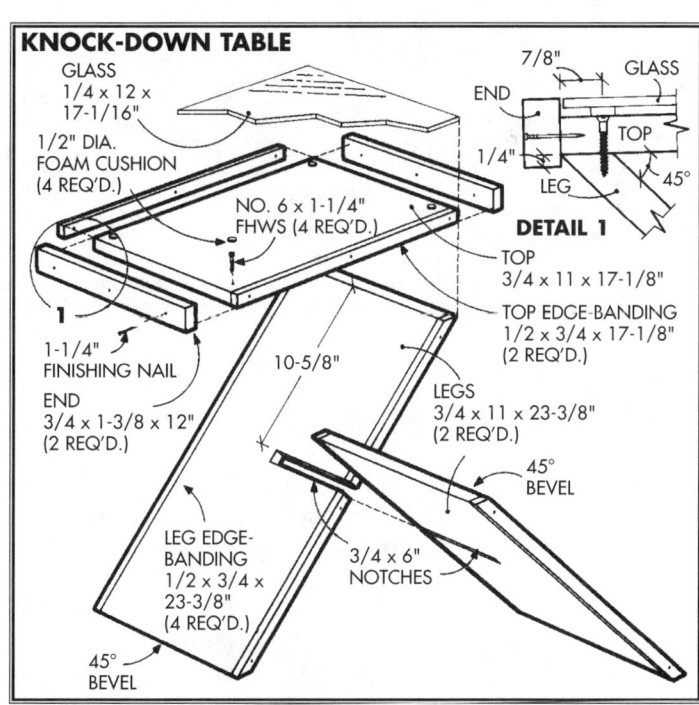

KNOCK-DOWN TABLE

Quick & Easy

TILE-TOP PLANT STAND

These tile-top plant stands were designed to take advantage of small leftovers from other projects. You can make them as gifts or to sell at local flea markets and crafts fairs.

This simple table with a ceramic tile inlay was designed to make use of small pieces of oak cabinet face. Its construction is simple, and the cost for materials (not including the wood) is only about $5.

The crowning touch on this table is the decorative tile. At local tile outlet stores, you can often find closeouts for just a fraction of the regular price — there's too little tile for most jobs but plenty for this project.

The frame for the top is 3/4- x 1-1/2-in. oak. (Any hard wood would be suitable for this project.) The size of the top is determined by the size of the tiles you use, so buy the tiles first and lay them out, allowing about 1/8

FURNITURE AND STORAGE PROJECTS

TILE-TOP PLANT STAND

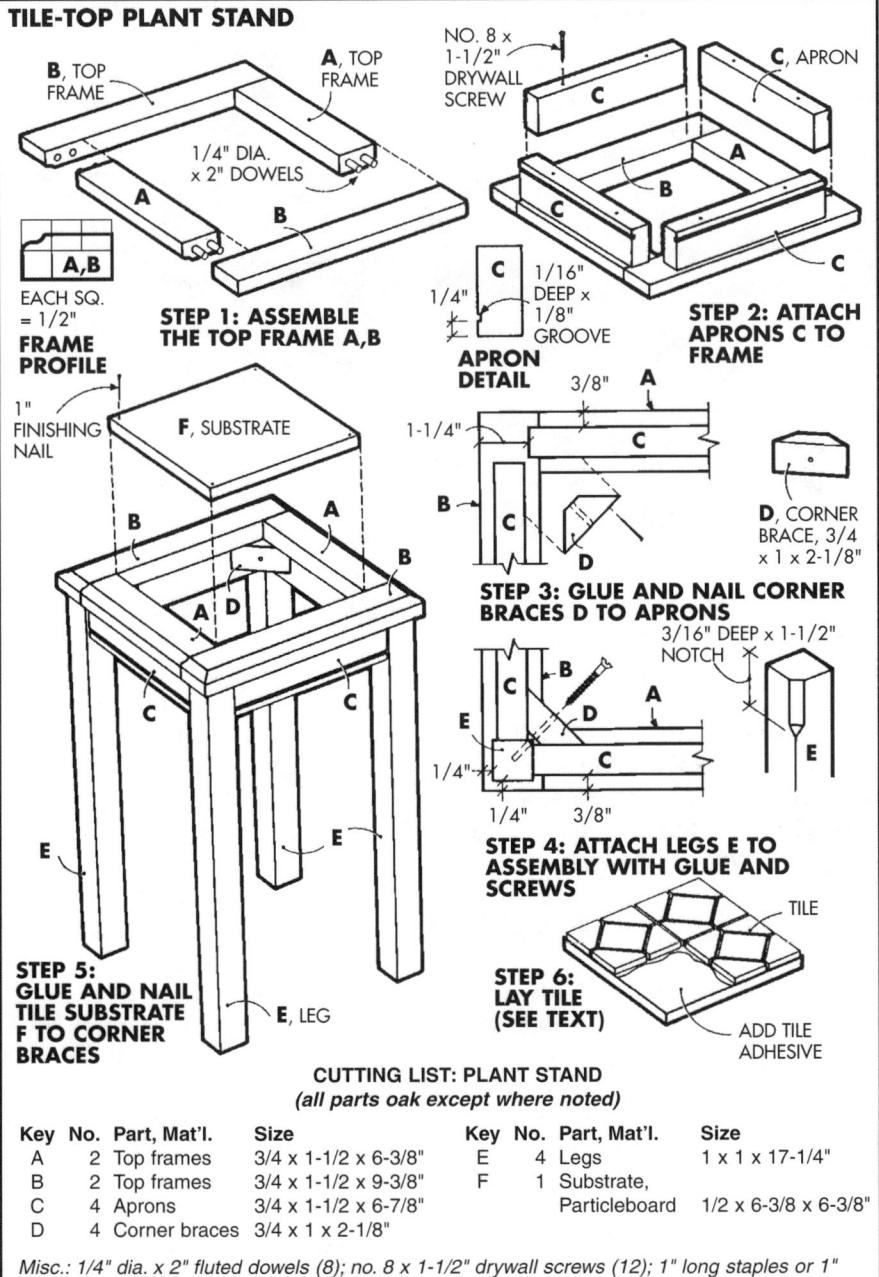

CUTTING LIST: PLANT STAND
(all parts oak except where noted)

Key	No.	Part, Mat'l.	Size
A	2	Top frames	3/4 x 1-1/2 x 6-3/8"
B	2	Top frames	3/4 x 1-1/2 x 9-3/8"
C	4	Aprons	3/4 x 1-1/2 x 6-7/8"
D	4	Corner braces	3/4 x 1 x 2-1/8"
E	4	Legs	1 x 1 x 17-1/4"
F	1	Substrate, Particleboard	1/2 x 6-3/8 x 6-3/8"

Misc.: 1/4" dia. x 2" fluted dowels (8); no. 8 x 1-1/2" drywall screws (12); 1" long staples or 1" wood screws (8); 1/4" thick ceramic tiles; ceramic tile adhesive and grout.

Attach the aprons to the underside of the frame with glue and screws in 1/2-in.-deep counter-bored holes.

in. for the grout around each tile.

Begin by cutting the frame pieces **A,B** to length and width (see cutting list, p. 45); then drill 1/4-in.-dia. x 1-1/16-in.-deep holes for the dowels. The quickest way to do this is to use a doweling jig; dowel centers with a drill press or a drill-alignment device will work, but they are quite a bit slower. As with any doweling operation, precise positioning of the holes and true perpendicular drilling are essential for an exact fit.

Assemble the frame **A,B** using yellow glue such as Titebond. It holds well and wipes clean with a damp cloth. Be sure to clean up all glue residue immediately or sand it off later to prevent splotchy, uneven staining.

Apply glue inside the holes and drive the 1/4-in.-dia. x 2-in. dowels into the frame pieces **A** with a rubber mallet. Multigroove (fluted) dowels are better than spiral-groove dowels for this operation. Multigroove dowels hold tight in woods of different densities — they press evenly into soft woods such as soft maple and poplar but cut their way into hard woods such as oak, cherry and walnut. Next, be sure all pieces fit exactly square and clamp them securely. Set the frame aside to let the glue dry.

Cut the aprons **C** next. The aprons should be 2-1/2 in. shorter than the length of the assembled frame. This allows the frame to overhang the 1-in.-sq. legs by 1/4 in. on each side.

Drill 3/32-in. pilot holes and 1/2-in.-deep counterbores for the no. 8 x 1-1/2-in. drywall screws in the aprons (see photo above). Drill the holes 1-1/2 in. from each end and centered on the edge (see drawing, step 2).

As a decorative touch, you can add a 1/8-in.-wide groove parallel to the bottom edge of the aprons. Use a

FURNITURE AND STORAGE PROJECTS

router with a 1/8-in. straight bit or a table saw set to a very shallow depth (1/16 in.). A small radius bead would also look attractive.

When the glued tabletop frame is dry, plane or sand each side square and rout a decorative edge. An ogee or Roman ogee bit cuts an attractive edge — use a scrap to experiment with various profiles until you find the style you like. After you finish routing, sand the underside of the frame with a belt sander.

Next, attach the four aprons **C** to the underside of the tabletop assembly. Glue and screw each rail centered on each side. Fasten with no. 8 x 1-1/2-in. drywall screws and allow the glue to set.

The corner braces **D** serve as mountings for the legs and top substrate. Cut them to length in a miter box or on a power saw that cuts 45-degree miters. Before you attach the braces, drill a 1/8-in.-dia. clearance hole and countersink through the middle of each brace for the leg mounting screw. (There is little clearance for the drill after you've attached the brace.)

Attach the corner braces **D** to the aprons flush against the underside of the top (see drawing, step 3). Be sure the braces are centered on each corner and that they fit tightly against the aprons. If you have an air compressor, use an air-powered stapler and glue to mount the braces. Use 1-in. staples with a 1/4-in. crown. Test the stapler on scrap wood to determine the proper air pressure. Too much pressure may drive the staple too far into the brace or even through to the outside of the apron. If you don't have an air-powered stapler, drill pilot holes, apply glue and mount the braces using 1-in. wood screws.

Cut the legs **E** to size next; then cut a 1-1/2-in.-long x 3/16-in.-deep stopped chamfer on the inside top corner of each leg. This provides a flat surface on which to drill and insert the mounting screw for the leg.

Next, attach the legs using the clearance holes in the braces to guide the no. 8 x 1-1/2-in. drywall screws (see drawing, step 4). Because there is little clearance for a drill under the table to bore through the brace into the leg, mark the entrance point on the leg and drill the pilot hole separately. Don't glue the legs on if you want to be able to remove them for any future purpose, such as changing the height of the table or moving.

Finally, measure the exact inside dimensions of the tabletop frame and cut the substrate **F** for the tile inlay, which is made from a scrap piece of 1/2-in.-thick high-density particleboard. The thickness of the tile determines the thickness of the substrate. (Almost all of the tile you'll find that's suitable for this project is 1/4 in. thick.) Cut and fit the substrate into the tabletop. Glue and nail or staple the substrate to the corner braces.

Now is the time to sand, stain and finish the table. A well-finished surface will be easier to clean after you apply grout to the tile. If you are using oak, it is especially important to finish before applying the grout, as the alkaline in the grout will darken the oak.

Sand all surfaces with 220-grit sandpaper, preferably using a random-orbit or oscillating finishing sander. Check that you've eliminated all scratches and swirl marks. Then finish the table with stain and two coats of varnish, sanding between coats.

After the finish on the table has cured, install the tile with ceramic tile adhesive. Apply the adhesive with a small 1/8-in. V-notched trowel. Set the tile and wiggle it slightly from side to side to be sure the adhesive makes good contact with the tile. Allow the tile to set for two days before you apply the grout.

White, gray or tan grout complements any tile. Use a latex grout additive to give the grout better flexibility and stain resistance. Follow the mixing instructions on the package carefully.

Apply the grout with a grout float or a flat flexible spatula. When the film on the tile just begins to dry, wipe diagonally across the grout lines with a moist terry cloth towel. (Some tile installers use a sponge to wipe the grout, but I have never found a sponge that creates grout lines as smooth as terry cloth does.) Rinse and wring out the towel and repeat, making each stroke lighter than the last, until you have removed all the grout from the tile surface and are left with clean, smooth grout lines. Make one final polish with a clean, dry towel after the grout has set up slightly — usually about 15 minutes.

After the grout has cured for three or four weeks, apply a sealer to resist stains and mildew.

Quick & Easy 49

PROJECTS FOR THE HOME OFFICE

Quick & Easy

4 DESK ACCESSORIES

Build a matching set of desk accessories to keep your office neat.

This four-piece set of colorful desk accessories adds a contemporary look to your home office and makes organizing your desk a pleasure. You need only basic woodworking skills to make the desktop file, bookends, pencil box and notepad holder.

1 NOTEPAD HOLDER
Designed to hold 1-1/2- x 2-in. and 3- x 4-in. notepads and a pen, the holder ensures you'll always be able to take a message without having to dig around for something to write on. The front, back, sides and divider are made of 1/4-in.-thick birch; the bottom pieces are made of 1/2-in. plywood.

Cut out the sides and the divider with a band saw or a scroll saw. Make the front and back about 1/16 in. wider than the finished dimension shown in the drawing, right; you'll sand off the excess material later. Cut two 3/8-in.-deep scoops in the front to access the note pads. Glue and clamp all pieces,

PROJECTS FOR THE HOME OFFICE

The holder keeps self-adhesive notepads neat and within reach.

making sure the bottom edges are flush.

Cut the bottom pieces to size and glue them in place. After the glue has dried, sand the top edge of the back and front flush with the sides using a belt sander. Sand the entire assembly, easing all edges, with 150-grit or finer sandpaper.

Cut a rectangular block for the pen holder. Fit the block in place and mark the taper even with the top of the side and divider; then cut along the lines with a band saw.

Next, bore the 3/8-in.-dia. hole for the pen. Sand the block and paint the top and front with blue semigloss alkyd enamel. Paint the rest of the holder burgundy. Glue the pen holder in place; then finish the entire holder with a coat of clear varnish.

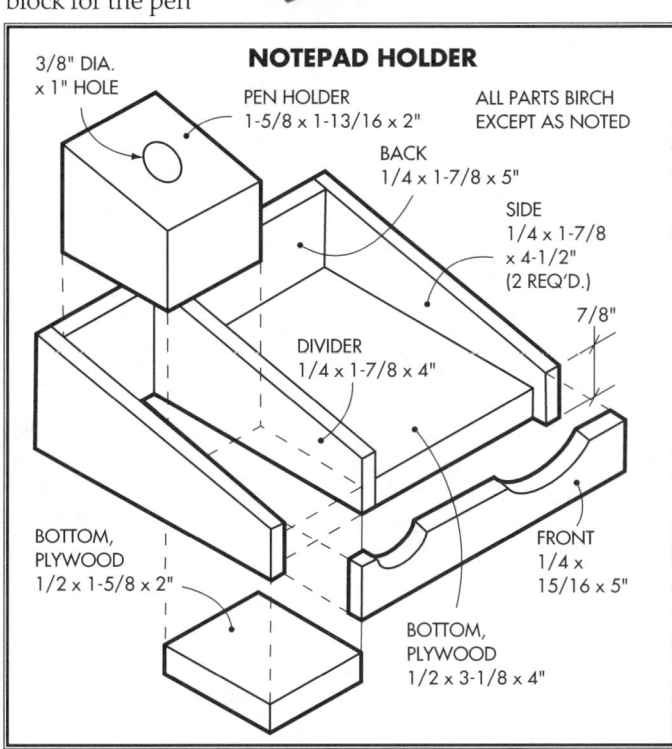

NOTEPAD HOLDER

3/8" DIA. x 1" HOLE

PEN HOLDER
1-5/8 x 1-13/16 x 2"

ALL PARTS BIRCH EXCEPT AS NOTED

BACK
1/4 x 1-7/8 x 5"

SIDE
1/4 x 1-7/8 x 4-1/2"
(2 REQ'D.)

7/8"

DIVIDER
1/4 x 1-7/8 x 4"

BOTTOM, PLYWOOD
1/2 x 1-5/8 x 2"

FRONT
1/4 x 15/16 x 5"

BOTTOM, PLYWOOD
1/2 x 3-1/8 x 4"

2 DESKTOP FILE

Using brazing rods and dowels, you can easily assemble a file holder to keep important information at your fingertips. The file is also great for storing your old record albums.

Start by cutting two 1-1/4-in.-dia. birch dowels to length in a miter box with a backsaw or with a circular saw. Never cut a dowel rod freehand with a power saw; always secure it in a miter gauge or cradle it in a block with a V-groove to prevent kickback.

To flatten the bottom of each dowel so it sits flat, secure the dowel in a bench vise and use a hand plane or a belt sander. Next, mark and bore the 1/8-in.-dia. x 1/4-in.-deep holes

Make this file holder from brass brazing rods and wood dowels.

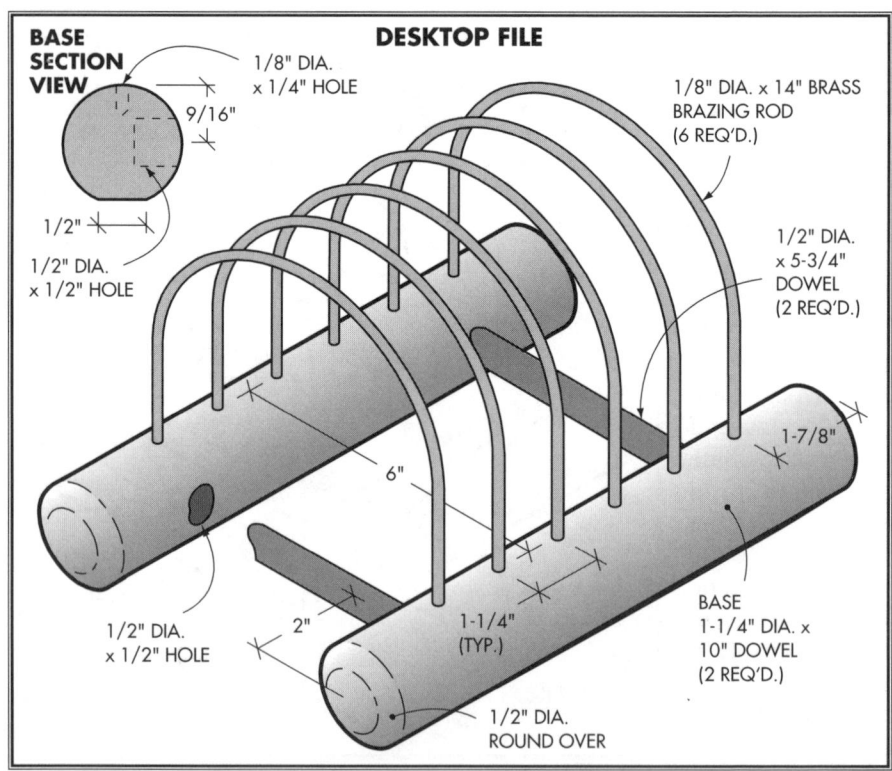

DESKTOP FILE

BASE SECTION VIEW
1/8" DIA. x 1/4" HOLE
9/16"
1/2"
1/2" DIA. x 1/2" HOLE

1/8" DIA. x 14" BRASS BRAZING ROD (6 REQ'D.)

1/2" DIA. x 5-3/4" DOWEL (2 REQ'D.)

1-7/8"
6"
1-1/4" (TYP.)

1/2" DIA. x 1/2" HOLE
2"

BASE 1-1/4" DIA. x 10" DOWEL (2 REQ'D.)

1/2" DIA. ROUND OVER

PROJECTS FOR THE HOME OFFICE

for the brazing rods with a drill press. (You can use a hand drill, but keep the drill bit perpendicular to the rod as you bore.) Then mark and bore the holes for the 1/2-in.-dia. connecting dowels. Clamp the dowel in a wooden handscrew while drilling to stabilize it and ensure the hole is straight.

Round the ends of the 1-1/4-in.-dia. dowels with a belt sander or by hand with sandpaper or a wood file. Cut the 1/2-in.-dia. dowels to length and sand all the wooden parts smooth with 150-grit sandpaper.

Paint the 1-1/4-in.-dia. dowels with semigloss alkyd enamel or lacquer. After the paint has dried, glue the connecting dowels in place. Finish with clear varnish or lacquer. (Don't mix the two types of finishes.)

Make a 5-in.-dia. circle out of 3/4-in. plywood or solid stock for bending the 1/8-in.-dia. brass brazing rods. (Note: If you can't find brazing rod, you can use coat hangers or any bendable 1/8-in.-dia. rod. Be sure to buy non-fluxed brazing rod.) Cut six 14-in. lengths of rod with heavy wire cutters or a hacksaw. Starting from one end, bend the rod around the form. Once inserted into the base, the rod will hold its shape. Polish the rods to a high luster; then coat with a clear finish to preserve the shine.

Shown in Color on Page 6

• •

3 PENCIL BOX

All you need to make the pencil box is one 1/4- x 3- x 48-in. piece of birch and a 3/4- x 30-in. half-round. The top can be glued together from 1/4-in.-thick stock, or you can use 3/4-in.-thick stock.

Begin by cutting the bottom to size (see drawing, p. 54); then cut the sides to fit around the bottom. Make the sides slightly oversize to allow for the miters. A power miter saw or table saw works best for cutting miters. Cut the first miter; then mark the second miter where it aligns with the end of the bottom.

After all the miters have been cut, apply glue to the miters and to the edges of the bottom. Assemble the sides around the bottom and clamp the box with rubber bands. The box has a tendency to pull in around the open top, so cut a few 2-1/2-in. scraps and insert them as braces in the opening.

Cut the stock for the top to size;

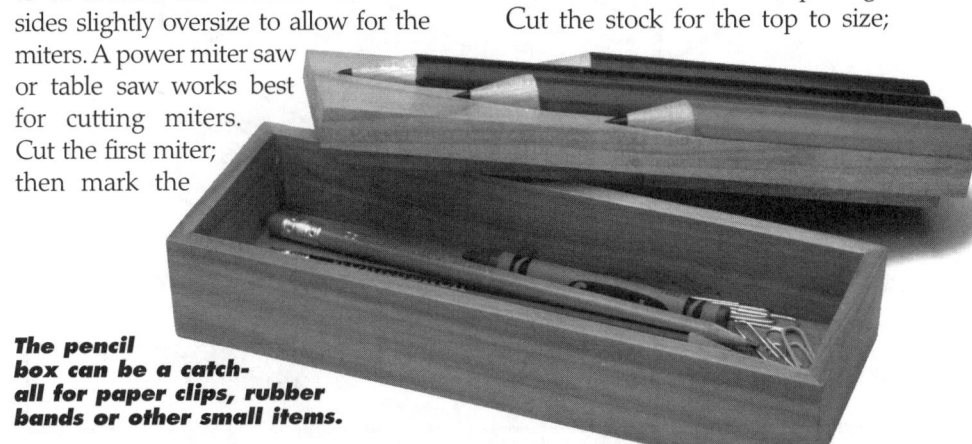

The pencil box can be a catch-all for paper clips, rubber bands or other small items.

then use a table saw or router to cut the 1/4- x 5/16-in. rabbet in all four edges. If you use a table saw, make the 5/16-in.-deep cuts in the edges first; then make the 1/4-in.-deep cuts in the bottom. This method is safer because it leaves more stock for support on the edge cuts.

Next, make the decorative pencils using half-round stock. You can make your own half-round from 3/4-in. stock using a 3/8-in. rounding over bit in a router mounted in a router table. Round over both edges of both sides;

then cut off the rounded edge with a band saw or a table saw. Cut the pieces to their finished length; then tape two pieces together back to back with one end flush. Rotate the stock on a belt sander to sharpen the flush ends to a point. You can also taper the ends with a file or a block plane.

Sand all parts smooth with 150-grit or finer sandpaper. Paint the pencils with semigloss alkyd enamel; then glue the pencils to the top and finish with a couple of coats of spray varnish.

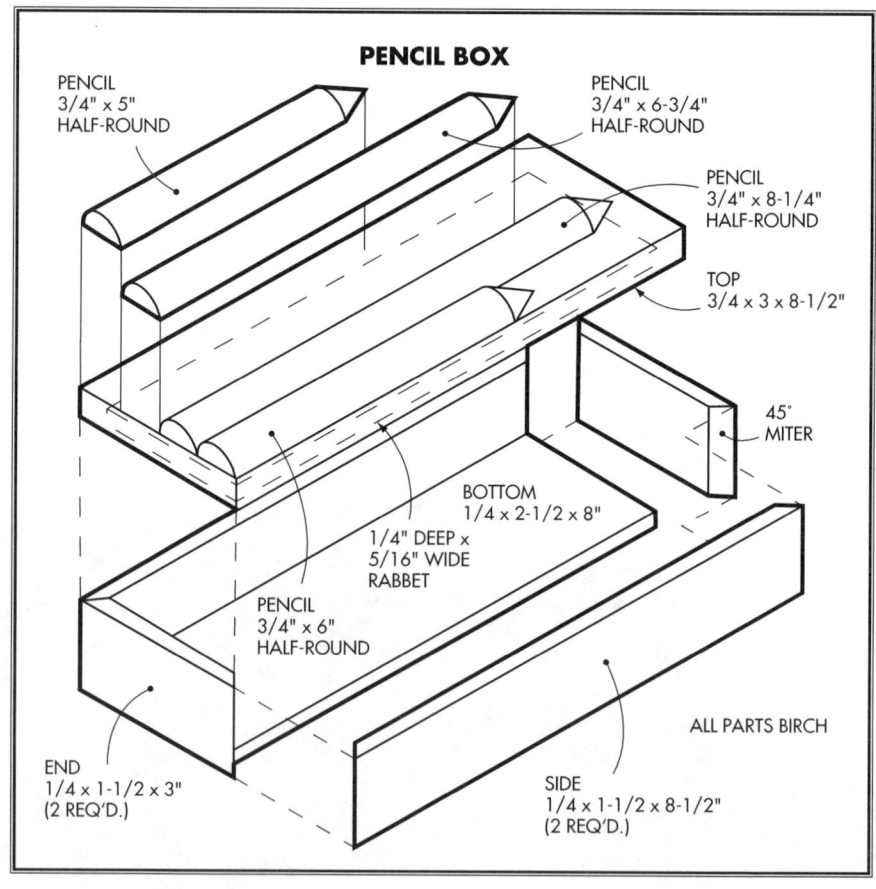

PROJECTS FOR THE HOME OFFICE

4 BOOKENDS

Metal base plates screwed to the bottom of these bookends make them sturdy enough to support several books.

Begin with a 1- x 5- x 36-in. piece of birch. Refer to the drawing on p. 56 to cut out the four books. Then round over the spines of the books using a hand plane or a router with a 3/8-in. rounding over bit.

Make the V-grooves that run along each side of the spine using a router with a veining bit. Use a router table for fast, safe cutting. If you don't have a router table, clamp a wooden straightedge to the workpiece or the router, and clamp the workpiece in place for safety.

Next, make the cuts across the spine with a thin-kerf handsaw or a band saw. Then make the 1/16-in.-deep notch in the bottom of both larger books to accept the metal base plate. A band saw, scroll saw or chisel are the safest tools to use for this cut. Don't use a table saw unless you have a sliding table that rides in the miter slots to support the workpiece.

If you have metal-cutting equipment, you can cut the base plates from 1/16-in.-thick metal. Ease the sharp edges of the plates with a file. Bore screw holes with a 1/8-in. metal-boring bit; then countersink the holes. Spray paint the top of the plates with flat black enamel.

Insert the base plates in the notches and mark the holes for the screws. Bore the screw holes (a no. 6 screw requires a 5/64-in.-dia. hole); then sand the books with 150-grit or finer sandpaper.

Paint the spines with semigloss alkyd enamel. When the paint is dry,

Shown in Color on Page 6

Sturdy wooden bookends can support a long row of books.

NOTE HOLDER

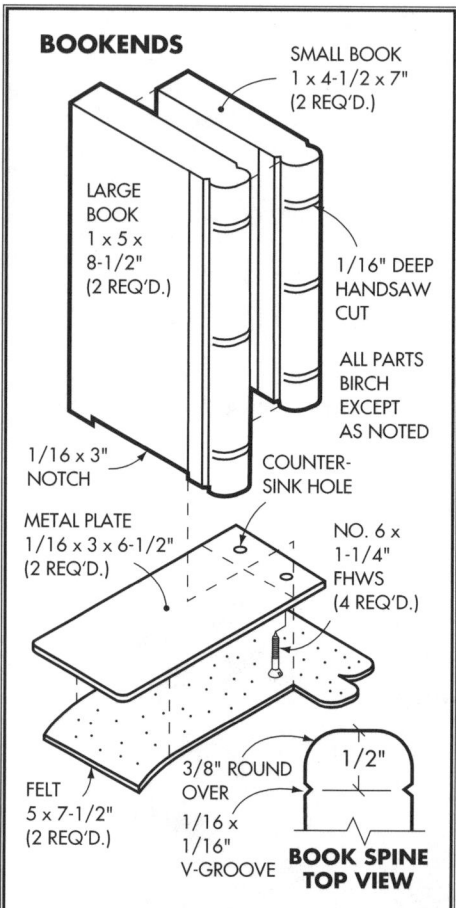

Message mongers take note: This handy holder is easier to use than a clamp-style clip because you can slip in a message with one hand. The secret is kids' stuff — a marble and the laws of gravity conspire to keep one small scrap of paper or several large pages firmly in place.

The holder shown is made out of ash, but any wood will do. Begin by cutting the base and clip to size (see drawing, opposite). Although it's easiest to do this with a band saw, you can use a table saw, but don't try to cut the pieces to length using the rip fence as a guide because the workpiece can bind and kick back. Instead, first rip the pieces to width (they should be at least a few inches longer than the diameter of the saw blade) and then use a miter gauge to crosscut them to length.

Next, use a band saw to cut the notch in the clip; then round over the outside edges of both pieces using a small block plane or sandpaper.

Cut the ramp for the marble using a sharp chisel. It must be smooth for the marble to roll easily, so sand it well. Before you glue the pieces

glue and clamp each small book to a larger book. Be sure the bottom and front edges are aligned. After the glue dries, apply two coats of spray varnish to complete the finish.

Screw the metal plates to the bottom of the books; then attach black felt to the bottom of the plates with contact cement or spray adhesive. Trim the felt with a sharp utility knife.

PROJECTS FOR THE HOME OFFICE

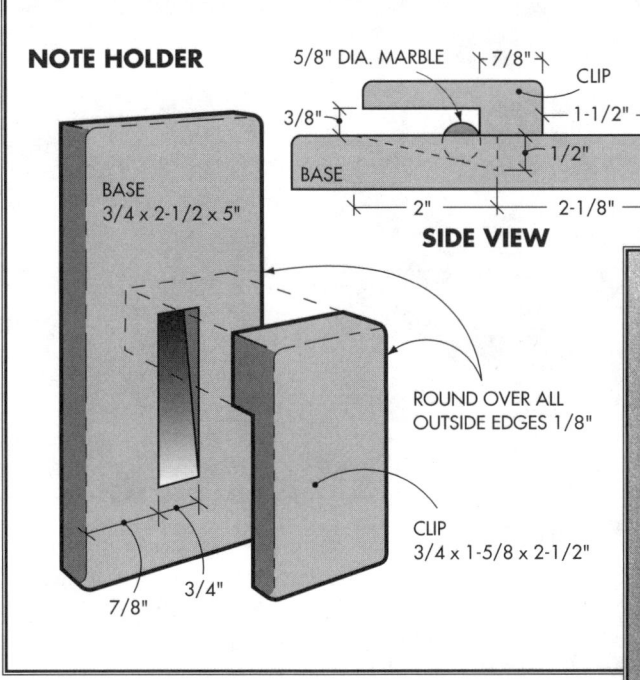

NOTE HOLDER

To leave a message, push the paper in from the bottom; to remove it, pull it out from the side.

together, set the marble in place, fit the clip against the base and hold the assembly upright. The marble should roll down and press against the clip. (You should be able to see about two-thirds of the marble.)

When you're satisfied with the fit, attach the clip to the base with glue and two 1-in. screws. Countersink the screw holes so the screw heads don't protrude when you hang the holder. Finally, attach magnets or a picture frame hanger or simply bore a hole through the top of the base for hanging.

MESSAGE CENTER

FAR RIGHT: A drawer in the message center holds pens, pencils and notepads. Use the back to post telephone messages.

NEAR RIGHT: To fasten the front and sides with an air nailer, angle the nailer back slightly and use a short nail that won't protrude through the front surface.

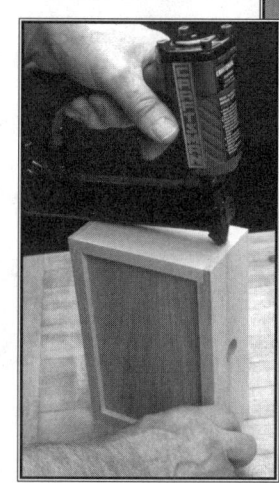

Using simple joinery and a brad nailer, you can make this message center in a few hours. The one shown is made of sycamore, but you can substitute any wood you like. Except for the back, which is 3/8 in. thick, all parts are made from 1/2-in.-thick stock. You can use 1/2-in. stock for all parts if you prefer, but you'll have to adjust the width of the top, the bottom and the rabbet joints in the sides.

Begin by cutting all the parts to exact size; then transfer the side and back curve patterns to the stock. Do not cut the curves yet, however; it's important to cut the rabbets and dadoes in the sides **A** first while the stock has square edges.

Lay out the joints in pencil on the sides **A**, the drawer front/back **D** and the drawer sides **E**. Cut the joints with a table saw or a router. Make all the 1/4-in.-deep cuts first, including the rabbets in the sides **A** and the grooves in the drawer sides **E** for the bottom **C**. Cut the dadoes in the sides **A** by making several passes over the table saw blade. Don't forget to bore the hole in the drawer front **D**.

When you've completed the joinery, cut the back and side curves with a band saw, sabre saw or scroll saw. If you use a band saw or sabre saw, you'll need to smooth the curves. Clamp the sides together in a bench vise so all the edges match and shape them with a rasp or file; then sand until the curve is smooth. Use the same method to smooth the back curve.

Check that all the parts fit together properly; then you're ready to assem-

PROJECTS FOR THE HOME OFFICE

MESSAGE CENTER

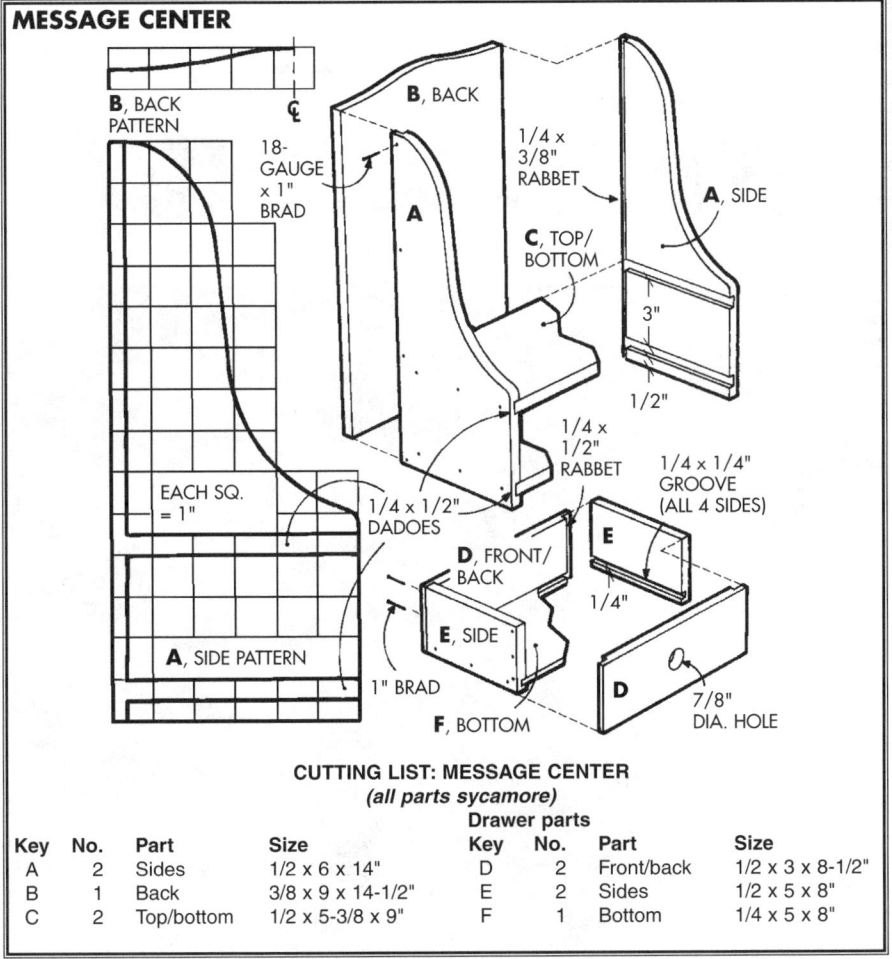

CUTTING LIST: MESSAGE CENTER
(all parts sycamore)

Key	No.	Part	Size	Key	No.	Part	Size
A	2	Sides	1/2 x 6 x 14"	D	2	Front/back	1/2 x 3 x 8-1/2"
B	1	Back	3/8 x 9 x 14-1/2"	E	2	Sides	1/2 x 5 x 8"
C	2	Top/bottom	1/2 x 5-3/8 x 9"	F	1	Bottom	1/4 x 5 x 8"

Drawer parts appear under the right-hand columns.

ble. Draw a line down the center of each dado or rabbet that you intend to nail through. This ensures that you won't have nails breaking though the surface of mating parts. Load your nailer with 1-in. brads; then apply glue to the joints. Always wear safety glasses when you nail — it's not uncommon for a nail to take an unplanned path. It's also a good idea to adjust the compressor's air pressure so the nailer sinks brads just below the surface. Hold the nailer parallel to the surface so that it's centered on the edge of the mating piece. When you nail the drawer sides to the front, angle the nailer slightly (see lower photo, opposite). Shoot one nail every 3 or 4 in.

When you're finished nailing, fill the nail holes with wood putty, and when they're dry, sand them flush with the surface. The message center shown was painted with white and blue alkyd enamel.

PLYWOOD WASTEBASKET

Slam-dunk your old memos into this bright yellow and blue wastebasket. Plywood construction makes the basket sturdy and provides enough weight so it's hard to tip over.

There's nothing that will improve your file 13 rim-shot accuracy like a brightly colored wastebasket. This basket requires a 24- x 36-in. piece of 1/4-in. plywood (this includes a little extra for waste), a 3/4- x 10- x 10-in. piece of plywood and a few small pieces of pine or poplar (see drawing, opposite). You'll need a router with a 1/4-in. straight bit, a sabre saw and a table saw or circular saw to complete the project.

Begin by laying out the sides on the plywood sheet. Mark a centerline for each side and measure from either side of the line to get the width for the top and bottom. Then draw lines to connect the top and bottom. First cut the sides to length; then cut the angles with a sabre saw or band saw.

Next, cut the 3/4-in.-thick bottom and mark the groove for the basket sides. Because the groove is stopped, it's best to use a plunge router to cut

PROJECTS FOR THE HOME OFFICE

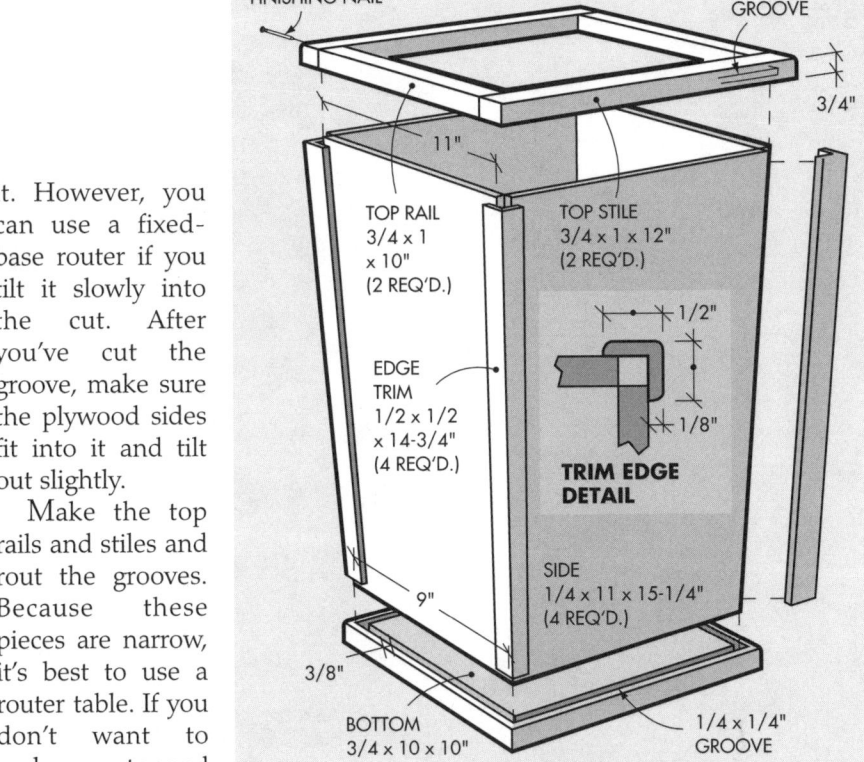

it. However, you can use a fixed-base router if you tilt it slowly into the cut. After you've cut the groove, make sure the plywood sides fit into it and tilt out slightly.

Make the top rails and stiles and rout the grooves. Because these pieces are narrow, it's best to use a router table. If you don't want to make a stopped groove in the stiles, you can plug the ends where the groove shows through after routing.

Glue and nail the rails and stiles together. End grain doesn't glue well — this is just a way to keep the parts together until you finish assembly.

You can make the edge trim as shown in the drawing, but it's a pretty tricky job. It's easier and safer to buy a similar corner molding at a home center. You could also glue lengths of dowel rod in the corners. Before assembly, round over all sharp corners.

To assemble, first glue the sides into the bottom grooves; then glue on the top. Finally, glue the trim onto the corners. If gaps show between the sides inside the basket, fill them with a paintable caulk.

Brush on a white primer coat before finishing with water-base enamel. Sand lightly between coats for a smooth finish. Let the paint dry for a few days before practicing your hook shots.

Quick & Easy

Quick & Easy
DECORATIVE ITEMS

Quick & Easy

HANGING QUILT RACK

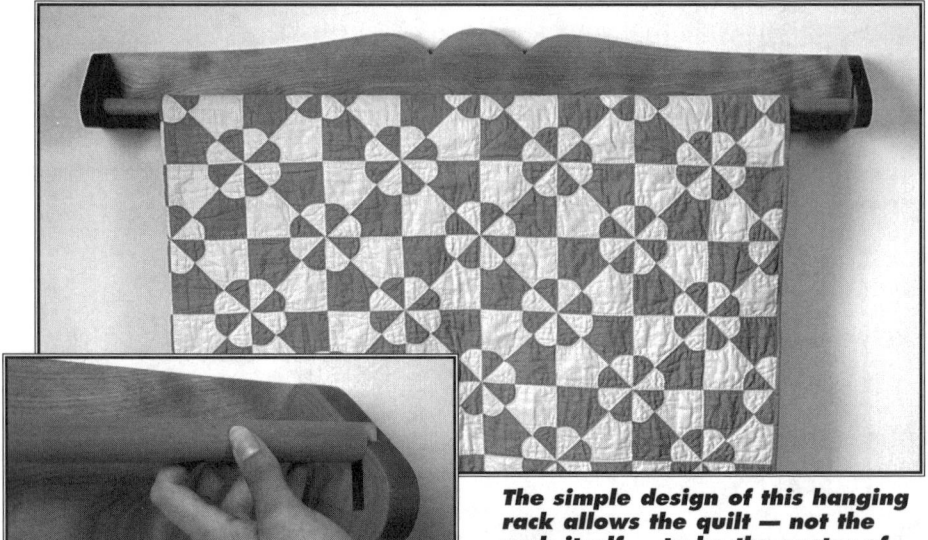

The simple design of this hanging rack allows the quilt — not the rack itself — to be the center of attention. The 1-in.-dia. dowel is notched to fit in slots in the ends so it won't roll.

This simple rack allows you to proudly display any size quilt. You can make the rack from any type of wood (the rack shown was made of birch) and finish it to suit your decor.

Begin by enlarging the end pattern and the back half-pattern to full size on a photocopier, or draw them full size on graph paper. Trace the patterns onto the stock, but don't cut them yet. It's best to cut the cleat groove in the back and the slot on the ends first.

The mating angled cleat and groove is a simple and secure way to hang the quilt rack without visible fasteners. Cut the cleat groove on a table saw. First cut a 1/2-in.-deep x 1-1/4-in.-wide groove; then change the blade angle to 45 degrees to make the angled cut on the top of the groove.

Next cut the slots for the hanger ends (see drawing). The best way to make the cut is with a router; then square the bottom of the cut with a

DECORATIVE ITEMS

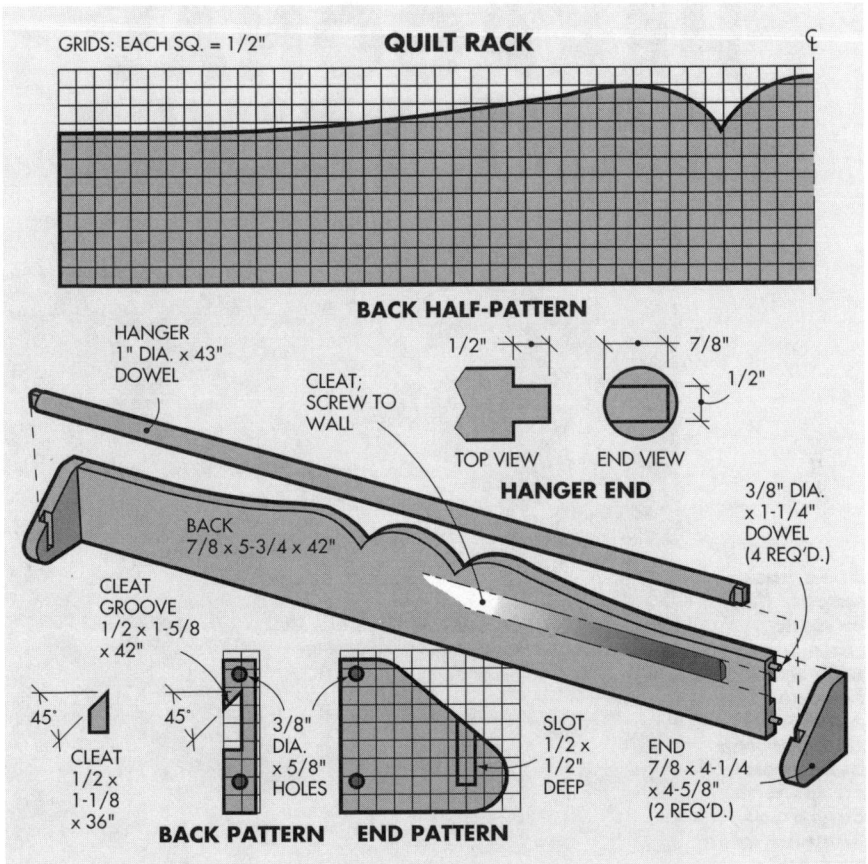

sharp chisel. Or use a chisel for the entire operation.

Now you can cut the ends and the back to shape with a band saw or sabre saw and sand the edges smooth. Notch the ends of the hanger dowel to make the tenons that fit into the end slots. It's important that the tenons be parallel or the hanger won't fit properly.

Next, bore the holes for the 3/8-in.-dia. dowels that connect the ends to the back. (If you have dowel centers, use them to align the holes.) Glue the dowels in the holes in the back; then glue and clamp the ends to the back. An easier method to join the back and ends is to attach them with counterbored screws and plug the holes.

To attach the cleat to the wall, drive drywall screws into the studs, or use hollow-wall fasteners. Slide the quilt rack onto the cleat; then slip the hanger into the slots and you're ready to display your favorite quilt.

HEXAGONAL PLANT TRIVET

Keep your carpet, floor or deck stain-free with this hexagonal plant trivet that you can build from scraps with only a saw, hammer, glue and nails.

Potted plants are an attractive addition to almost any setting, but they can leave some unattractive stains if the pot leaks or sweats. This plant trivet allows moisture to evaporate from underneath the pot and enhances the plant's appearance.

DECORATIVE ITEMS

Shown in Color on Page 7

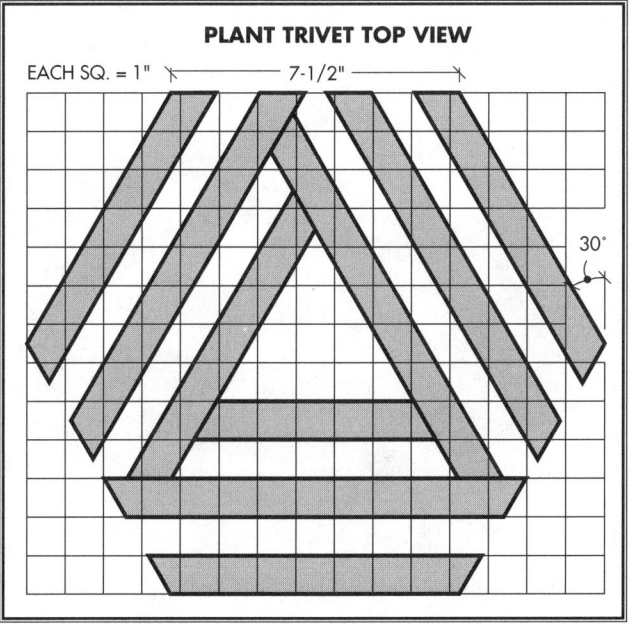

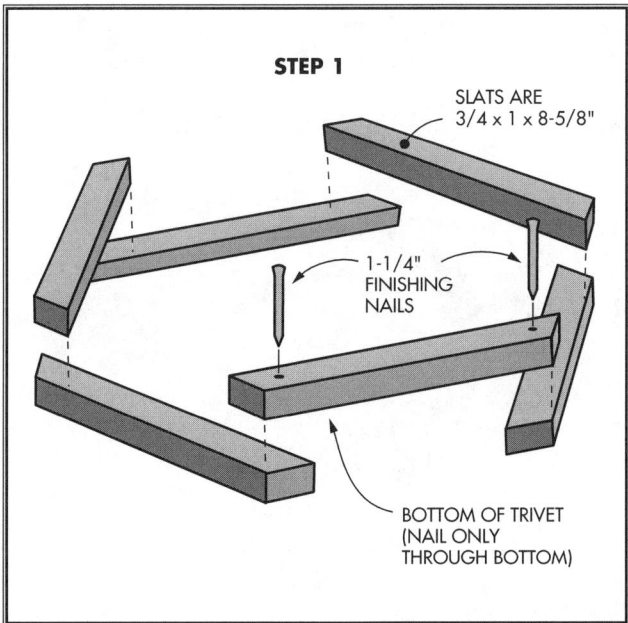

Although the trivet looks like it might be difficult to make, it's actually very easy. There are 18 pieces of three different lengths; all are 3/4 in. thick x 1 in. wide. Redwood or pressure-treated pine are the best choices.

First, draw a hexagon on newsprint, craft paper or cardboard using the pattern in the drawing. The hexagon for this trivet has 7-1/2-in. sides. Next, use a band saw or table saw to rip enough 1-in.-wide stock to make the number of trivets you want.

Cut all of the pieces a little longer than they need to be and then set your saw's miter gauge to 30 degrees. Cut the angle on one end of each piece and then turn the piece and cut the angle on the opposite side. Clamp a stop block on the saw fence to make repetitive cuts.

To assemble the trivet, work from the outside in toward the center. Use the hexagon drawing as an outside pattern to assemble the first course of 8-5/8-in. strips. Alternate every other strip — one on the top, then one on the bottom — gluing and nailing as you go. Drive the nails from only one side of the strips — that way all the nail holes will be on the bottom of the trivet.

Glue and nail the second course of strips using a spare strip as a spacer. Turn over the trivet and nail strips on the other side. The third and last course has one strip of each length. Start with the longest and work your way to the shortest. Alternate from top to bottom as you nail on each piece.

No finishing is necessary, but it doesn't hurt to sand the edges a bit and apply stain or water repellent.

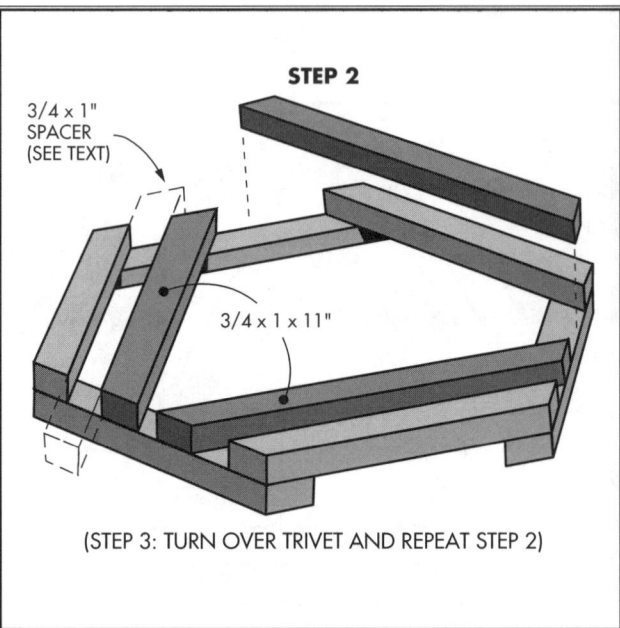

STEP 2

3/4 x 1" SPACER (SEE TEXT)

3/4 x 1 x 11"

(STEP 3: TURN OVER TRIVET AND REPEAT STEP 2)

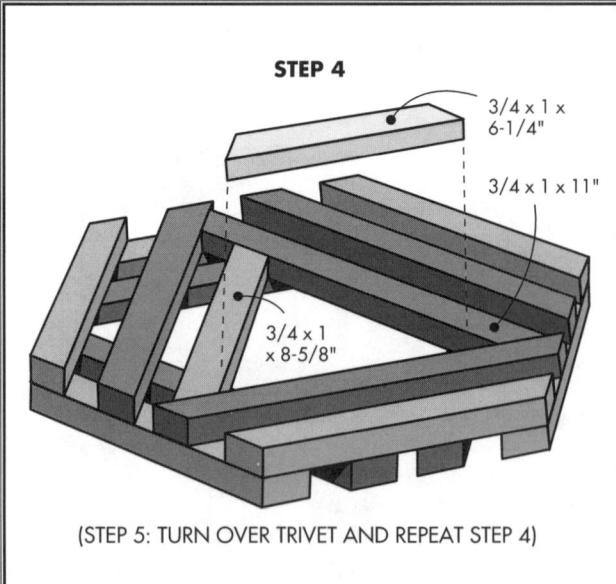

STEP 4

3/4 x 1 x 6-1/4"

3/4 x 1 x 11"

3/4 x 1 x 8-5/8"

(STEP 5: TURN OVER TRIVET AND REPEAT STEP 4)

DECORATIVE ITEMS

PLANT ORNAMENTS

Shown in Color on Page 7

Miniature birdhouses add a touch of color to houseplants and can be made from scraps.

Frustrated lawn ornament lovers will appreciate this project. If you live in an apartment or have already decked every square inch of your yard, don't despair — now you can decorate the vegetation inside your home.

All you need to make these faux birdhouses are some scraps of 3/4-in. stock, a few inches of 3/8-in. stock (lattice is perfect) and 1/8-in.-dia. dowels, cooking skewers or a coat hanger for the posts.

Start by cutting the 3/4-in. stock for the base to the size and shape you want. (Ours are 1-1/2 to 2-1/2 in. wide x 2-1/4 to 3 in. tall.) The rectangular birdhouses have 45-degree miters (accuracy is not important) cut at the top for the roofs; the other birdhouse is simply cut at a 45-degree angle. Cut the 3/8-in. stock for the roof so it overhangs the base 1/4 to 1/2 in.

To bore the holes for the post and perch, use a bit that's slightly larger than the diameter of the material you're using for the posts. It's a good idea to bore a few test holes in a scrap to make sure you have the right size bit before you drill into the base. Next, bore the entry hole in the front of the base with a 3/8-in. bit.

Paint all the pieces before assembly. The birdhouses in the photos have a realistic rough-hewn look — they weren't sanded, and the paint is thin and uneven. After the paint is dry, cut off a 3/8-in.-long piece of the post and insert it in the perch hole. Attach the roof with a single brad; then insert the post in the hole in the base. (If the fit is tight, you don't need to use glue.) All that's left is to nestle the house in the foliage of your favorite plant.

OCTAGONAL CLOCKS

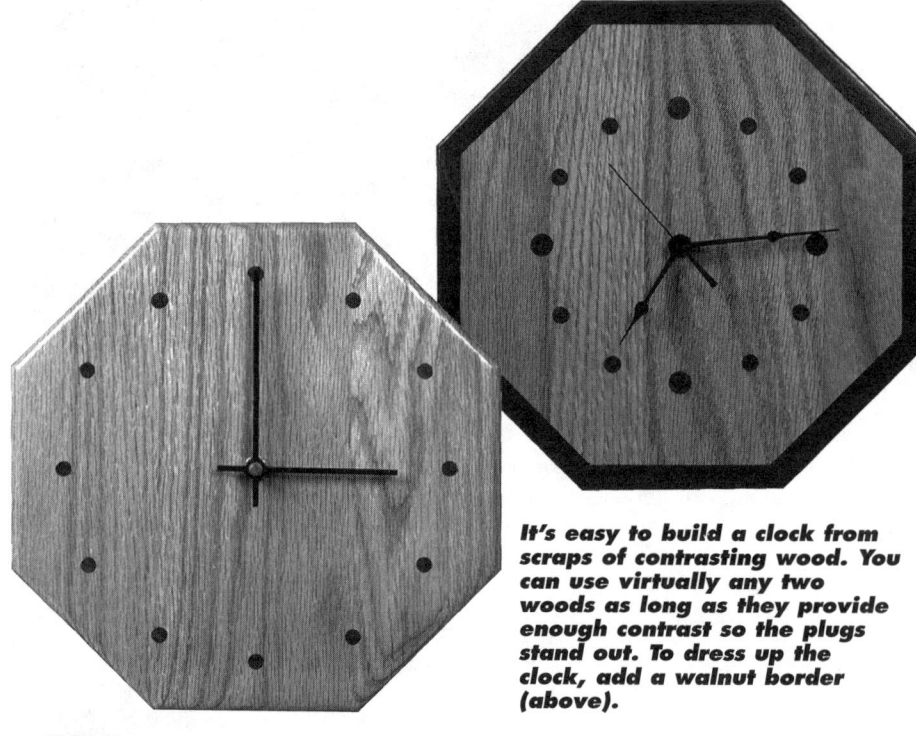

It's easy to build a clock from scraps of contrasting wood. You can use virtually any two woods as long as they provide enough contrast so the plugs stand out. To dress up the clock, add a walnut border (above).

A contemporary clock is easy to build from scraps lying around your shop. The clocks shown have oak bodies with walnut plugs to mark the hours. If you already have the necessary scraps on hand, an inexpensive battery-operated quartz clock movement will be your only expense for this project.

Make the clock body by edge-gluing several 2- to 4-in.-wide pieces of 3/4-in.-thick oak. For those who like to use dowels or biscuits to align the pieces, be sure to place them where they won't be exposed when you cut the clock shape. Once the glue dries, smooth the joints with a belt sander and a cabinet scraper.

DECORATIVE ITEMS

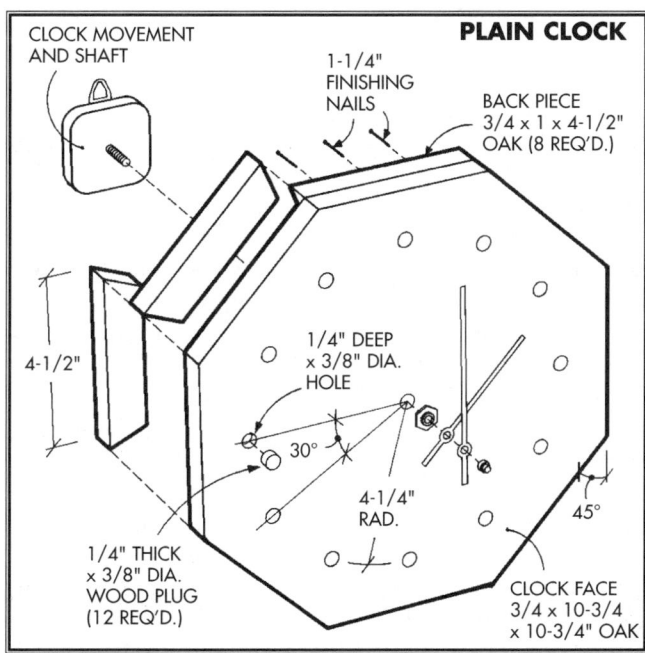

Cut the edge-glued blank into a 10-3/4-in. square. To find the center of the square, draw two diagonal lines from corner to corner. Use an awl to mark where the lines intersect.

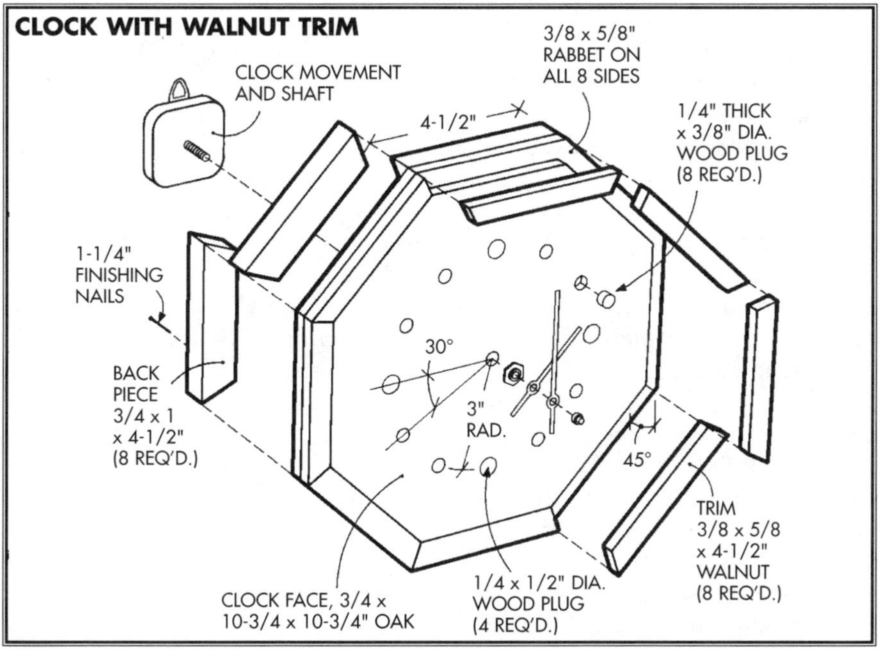

Now lay out an octagon with 4-1/2-in. sides using a combination square. Cut the octagon with a power miter saw, a radial arm saw or a table saw fitted with a miter gauge.

Next, measure and cut the eight 3/4-in.-thick x 1-in.-wide x 4-1/2-in.-long back pieces from oak. These pieces create a cavity for flush-mounting the quartz movement to the back of the clock body. Cut 22-1/2-degree miters at both ends of each piece.

Because the sides of the octagon may not be exactly the same, test the fit of the back pieces and make any adjustments before gluing. Secure the pieces with glue and 1-1/4-in. nails, or you can use just glue and clamps. Attach two opposite pieces at a time. The last two sides are the "shutters." A precise fit here will complete a nice, tight octagon with barely visible seams.

To make the optional 1/2-in.-walnut border around the clock face, cut a 3/8-in.-deep x 5/8-in.-wide rabbet around the edge of the clock face (see drawing). Cut eight pieces of 3/8- x 5/8- x 4-1/2-in. walnut; then cut a 22-1/2-degree miter on each end. As with the sides, be sure the fit of each piece is exact. Test the fit and then glue and clamp the pieces. Using a belt sander, sand each piece flush with the face and side.

Use a compass and the center hole you marked earlier to lay out the holes for the wood plugs. The distance from the center to the holes depends on the length of the hands — the minute hand should extend to the outside edge of the plug or slightly beyond. For the 4-1/4-in. straight hands (shown on the plain oak clock) lay out a circle with a 4-1/4-in. radius. For the 3-7/16-in. spade hands (shown on the clock with the walnut trim) lay out a circle with a 3-1/8-in. radius. Now use an inexpensive plastic 30-60-90 triangle to divide the clock face into 30-degree sections. You will bore the holes for the plugs where the 30-degree lines intersect the circle.

You can make all the plugs the same size or use different sizes. The clock with the walnut trim has 1/2-in.-dia. plugs for the hours 3, 6, 9 and 12 and 3/8-in. plugs for the remaining hours. The plain clock has 3/8-in.-dia. plugs.

Drill 1/4-in.-deep holes for all the plugs using a Forstner bit or a brad-point bit to avoid tearout. Next, cut the plugs. Self-ejecting plug cutters make this step easy. Apply glue and then tap each plug into place with a rubber mallet.

After the glue has set, sand the plugs flush with the clock face using a belt sander. A 1/4-in.-radius rounded edge looks nice.

Now bore a hole in the center of the clock face for the clock movement shaft. (Verify the diameter of the movement shaft before drilling this hole.)

Finally, sand with 220-grit sandpaper and apply two coats of varnish, sanding between coats. All that's left is to mount the quartz movement and the hands and your clock is ready to hang.

DECORATIVE ITEMS
PICTURE FRAMES

Shown in Color on Page 7

A 5x7 photo of Mickey Mouse inspired this frame. The 1/2-in.-thick pine circles are cut on a scroll saw and notched to fit the 1/2- x 2-1/2- x 7-in. pine base. Each circle is secured with adhesive caulk and a countersunk no. 5 x 1-in. flathead wood screw through the bottom of the base. A 3/4- x 3/4- x 7-in. pine cleat behind the photo is nailed and glued to the base to keep the photo in place. Glossy red paint completes the project.

In just a few hours you can design and build interesting picture frames in shapes to complement your favorite photos. All you need is 1/8-in.-thick acrylic, decorative adhesive tape, caulk, short dowels, wood scraps and some paint.

Some acrylic suppliers have scrap bins where you can find small pieces for low prices. If you do buy scraps, check to make sure the pieces aren't scratched. You can have the acrylic cut to size at the store or cut it yourself if you have a table saw with a carbide-

A 5x7 photo is sandwiched between 7/8-in.-dia. dowels from 2-5/8 to 8-1/2 in. long. The rear dowels are spaced 5/16 in. from the front dowels. The dowel on the far right is for decoration. The base is 3/4- x 2-3/4- x 6-1/2-in. pine. Each dowel is glued into a 1/2-in.-deep hole with adhesive caulk. After priming, spray on two or three coats of glossy black paint.

tipped blade. Make sure the blade is sharp; then feed the plastic slowly through the blade. (Wear full-face protection when cutting.) Cut the acrylic the exact size of the photo.

Sandwich the photo between the acrylic pieces and hold the pieces together with strong adhesive tape. The tape used on the frames in the photos is chrome automotive trim tape. Cut the tape into 1/2-in.-wide strips. This allows an overhang on

Four 3/4-in.-dia. dowels — two 2 in. long and two 3 in. long — surround a 3-1/2- x 5-in. photo. The dowels rest in 1/2-in.-deep holes in the 3/4- x 2- x 5-3/4-in. pine base. A 1/4- x 5/8- x 3-1/2-in. strip of wood is glued and nailed to the base behind the photo to keep it in place. Apply metallic gold spray paint after priming.

DECORATIVE ITEMS

This snapshot is nestled between 3/8-in.-dia. dowels of 3-1/2-, 4-1/2- and 5-1/2-in. lengths and a 3/4- x 3/4- x 5-1/2-in. pine cleat. The cleat is glued and nailed to the 5/16- x 2-1/2- x 5-1/2-in. base. Dowels are held with thin beads of adhesive caulk.

Shown in Color on Page 7

each side that you can trim later. Remove the tape's backing a little at a time as you wrap it around the acrylic. Start and end at the bottom to hide the seam.

After you've applied the tape, press it firmly in place with your fingers and trim the overhang using a utility knife with a sharp blade. Next, burnish the tape with a wood dowel. Don't use a screwdriver or other metal implement because metal will scratch the chrome surface.

Now that the photo has been mounted, you can design the stand to hold it. Keep in mind that there must be a front support and a rear support for the photo. Space the supports 5/16 in. apart to allow for the thickness of the acrylic, the photo and the paint.

If you're using dowels standing on end, make a 3/4-in.-thick base so you can bore 1/2-in.-deep holes with brad-point bits. Then all it takes is a few dabs of adhesive caulk to hold the dowels in the holes. (Unlike yellow glue, adhesive caulk doesn't require clamping pressure.) A few thin beads of the caulk are all you need to hold dowels that are lying down (see the frame in the photo above).

After you've assembled the stand, apply the finish of your choice. Spray on a sandable primer, let it dry (about 15 minutes) and sand with 400-grit sandpaper. Wood with prominent end grain or open pores may require a second or third coat of primer. The smooth, professional-looking finish the primer allows you to achieve is worth the extra time and effort. When you're satisfied with the primer, apply the paint. Once the finish is dry, slip the mounted photos in place.

LATHE-TURNED ORNAMENTS

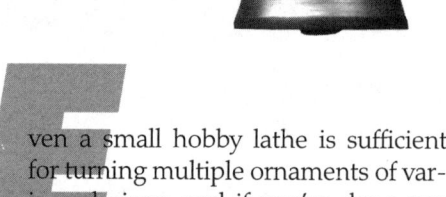

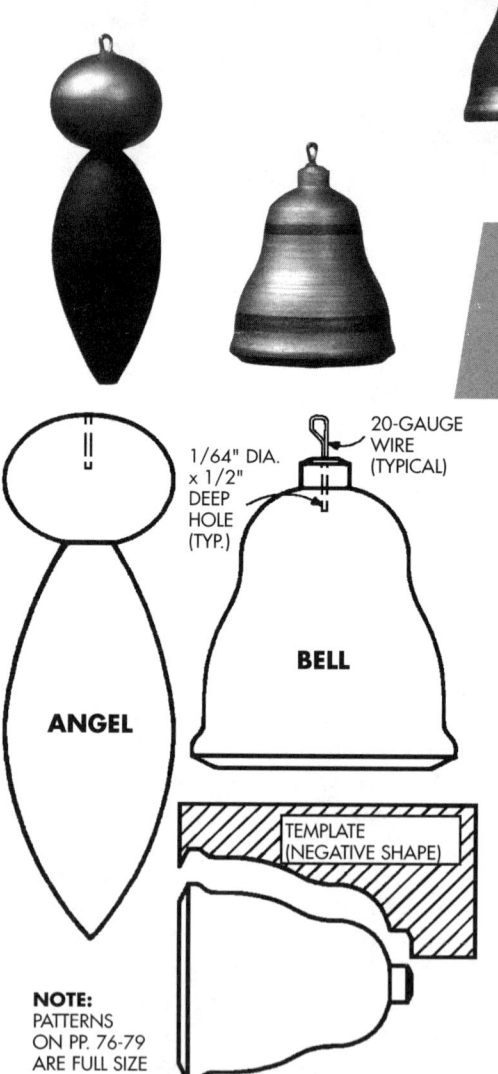

NOTE:
PATTERNS
ON PP. 76-79
ARE FULL SIZE

Even a small hobby lathe is sufficient for turning multiple ornaments of various designs, and if you've done any spindle turning at all, you'll have no trouble making them.

Depending on the size of the ornament and the length of your stock, you can turn two to six ornaments at a time. Turning goes quickly when you turn multiple ornaments.

Maple is the best wood for making the ornaments because it turns cleanly and holds fine details well. However, you can use other woods such as birch, beech or poplar.

Begin by cutting 6- to 8-in.-long square stock sections of a size that allows you to make several of the desired ornament. For instance, to make three acorns you'll need a piece of stock that's about 2 x 2 x 8 in. To make four bells, use a piece that's about 1-1/2 x 1-1/2 x 8 in.

You can turn square stock, but initial turning is much easier if you first

DECORATIVE ITEMS

Wooden Christmas tree ornaments have old-fashioned warmth that plastic and glass ornaments can't match. Use the patterns below and on p. 79 to turn similar ornaments, or design your own.

Shown in Color on Page 8

cut off the corners to make the stock octagonal. It's best to use a band saw with the table tilted 45 degrees. (Unless you're working with 12-in. or longer stock, the pieces are too small to be cut safely on a table saw.) Use the band saw to cut a shallow cross on one end of the workpiece for mounting it on the spur-center headstock.

Mount the workpiece in the lathe and adjust the tool rest to within 1/8 in. of the work. Turn the work by hand before starting the lathe to be sure the work doesn't hit the tool rest. Begin by roughing a cylinder with a gouge (photo 1, p. 78). For small spindle turnings like this you can run the lathe at a fairly high speed (1,000 to 1,500 rpm). Test for flat spots on the cylinder by laying the gouge shaft on

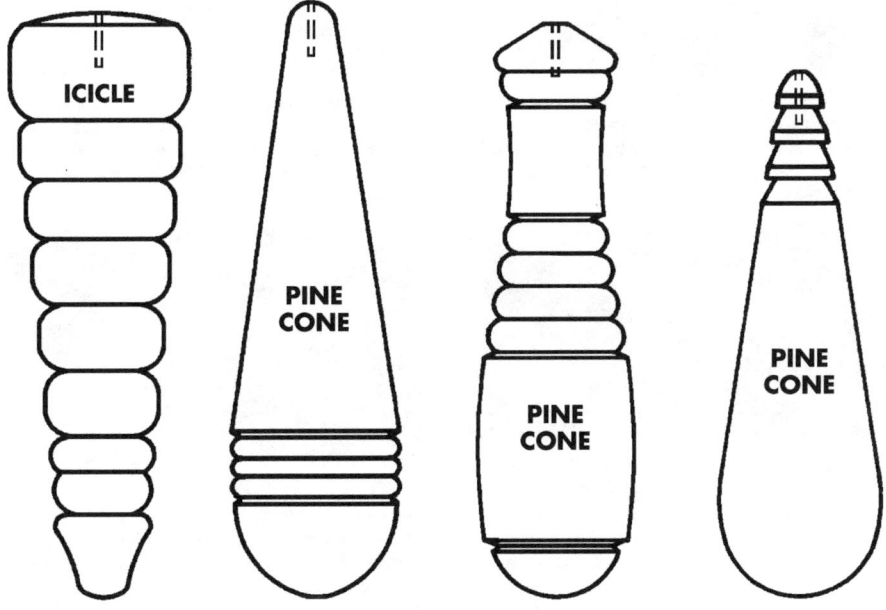

top of the spinning work. If the gouge doesn't bounce or chatter, you know that the cylinder is round.

Now you need to think about transferring the ornament pattern shapes to the work. There are two simple ways to accomplish this. Use outside calipers to measure and transfer dimensions directly from the full-size patterns. Start with the largest diameters and work your way to the smallest as you turn. Or make cardboard templates from the patterns. Just trace around half of the pattern (lengthwise) on card stock; then cut out the shape of the ornament with a craft knife (see bell pattern drawing).

Check accuracy by fitting the negative shape of the cardboard over the work as you turn. You don't need to make exact reproductions of the patterns. If the ornaments look good to you, that's all that matters.

With a parting tool, make entry cuts in the cylinder spaced slightly farther apart than the length of the ornaments (photo 2). Don't make the cuts too deep or the stock won't have enough strength to prevent it from chattering, whipping or breaking when you apply tool pressure.

Begin shaping the ornaments with a gouge or skew (photo 3). Work on the ornaments as a group in stages. Don't

HOW TO TURN FOUR BELLS AT ONCE

1 First chuck a 6- to 8-in.-long octagonal piece in the lathe. Next, use a small gouge or skew chisel to turn the piece into a cylinder.

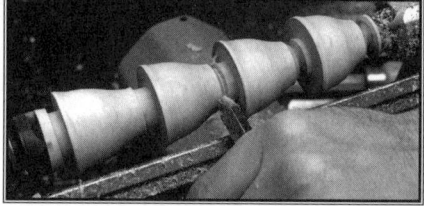

3 Rough out the shape with a gouge and scraper using templates or measuring with calipers. Keep the tool rest close to the work.

2 Mark divisions slightly longer than the finished length of the ornaments (bells in this case); then make entry cuts with a parting tool. Don't make the cuts too deep.

4 Clean up the work as much as possible; then pare the bell tops down to a small diameter. Make light cuts — you can easily break the work.

try to complete one and move on to another. Start with basic shapes; then work into the details. For instance, when you're turning the bells, make cone shapes first; then add the curves. Use calipers or the template to check the shape. Because the template won't fit over the work at this point, just put it behind the work and sight along the top of the turning.

Continue shaping the ornaments until they're refined to your satisfaction. You'll need to make lighter cuts as you near completion. Now use a parting tool or skew to reduce the stock to the smallest diameter, such as around the top of the bell (photo 4). Start at the tailstock and work your way to the headstock. Be very careful — if the connection between ornaments gets too small, they can be twisted apart by the lathe's torque. You'll experience a certain amount of chatter as the connection becomes smaller, but this is normal. Finish the turning by lightly sanding (photo 5).

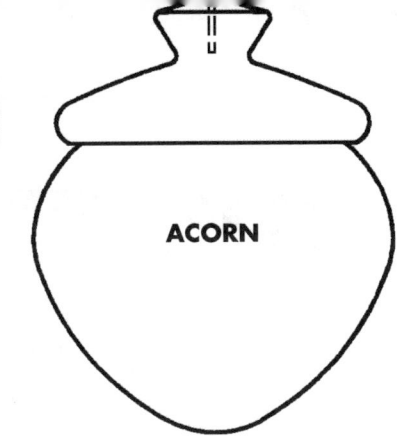

ACORN

The ornaments shown were finished on the lathe with indelible markers in traditional colors and gold and silver metallic markers.

Use the tool rest to support the markers and slowly paint the ornaments from one end to the other (photo 6). Depending on the color and the brand of the marker, you may need to coat an ornament two or more times.

After the ink is dry, remove the stock from the lathe and cut apart the individual ornaments with a coping saw. Then pare the rough edges smooth with a knife and touch up the wood.

To make a loop for hanging the ornament, bore a 1/64-in.-dia. x 1/2-in.-deep hole in the top (see drawing). Cut a piece of 20-gauge wire 1-1/4 in. long and double it over. Put a small amount of epoxy glue in the hole; then push the wire into the hole.

When the glue has dried, open up the wire loop and tie on string or wire.

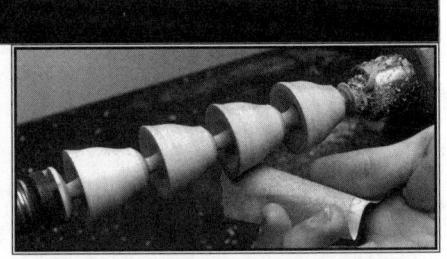

5 When you can refine the bells no further with cutting tools, switch to sandpaper. Sand from the bottom side, as shown here, for the best control. There's no need to use more than 150-grit paper.

6 Brace the marker on the tool rest to achieve smooth results. Experiment with different colors and various point sizes.

Quick & Easy

COUNTRY WALL HANGING

You don't have to be a master painter to create rustic wall hangings like this one. Using rough-cut 1/4-in.-thick x 1-3/8-in.-wide strips of wood and water-base acrylic paints, you can easily create your own lath art.

Wood lath was used as the backing for plaster walls in older buildings. You may be able to find lath where old buildings are being remodeled or torn down, or you can buy new lath at a lumberyard. You can also resaw your own strips from 3/4-in. stock.

Typical lath creations range in size from 8 x 8 in. to 30 x 40 in. The 7-1/2- x 9-7/8-in. (not counting the frame) country house is a good size for learning the technique. Start with an 8- x 12-in. piece of 1/4-in. plywood for the backing **H**. The exact size isn't critical as long as it's larger than the finished size. You'll trim it later.

Cut the lath to size as shown in the cutting list. Except for the roof and the sky triangles, only square cuts are required. The lath is easily cut with a handsaw, but a miter box and a backsaw ensure you'll get a 90-degree cut. To make the roof **D**, make end cuts at 60 degrees; then use the cutoffs for the triangles **E**.

After cutting the lath pieces to size, fit them together without glue according to the pattern. Make any necessary

This folksy wall hanging is made of rough-sawn lath salvaged from old plaster walls and painted with water-base acrylic paints.

adjustments to ensure a snug fit. Glue the sawn pieces to the backing using construction adhesive, yellow glue or hot-melt glue.

Start with the ground **A**. Apply glue to the back of the lath. If you're using yellow glue, allow it to set until it is slightly tacky; then lay the piece in one corner of the backing. Glue the left-hand piece **B** flush with the left edge of

DECORATIVE ITEMS

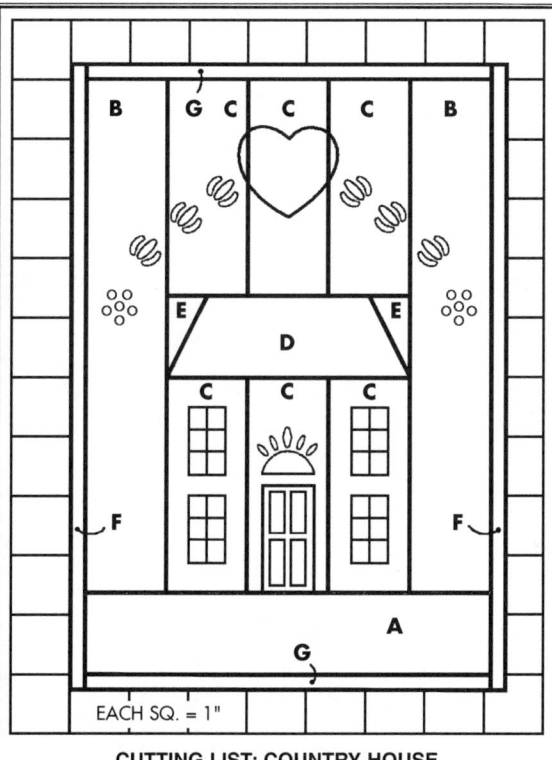

CUTTING LIST: COUNTRY HOUSE
(all parts 1/4" thick rough-sawn lath except as noted)

Key	No.	Part, Mat'l.	Size*
A	1	Ground	1-3/8 x 7-1/2"
B	2	Background and sky	1-3/8 x 8-1/2"
C	6	House and sky	1-3/8 x 3-1/2"
D	1	Roof	1-3/8 x 4-1/2"
E	2	Sky triangles	3/4 x 1-3/8" (cutoffs from roof)
F	2	Frame sides	1-3/8 x 10-3/8"
G	2	Frame top/bottom	1-3/8 x 7-1/2"
H	1	Backing, plywood	1/4 x 8 x 12" (trim after gluing)

*Adjust to fit according to width of lath.

Shown in Color on Page 8

paper in case you have glue squeeze-out, lay a piece of plywood on top of the paper and then add the weights (books or bricks). Allow the glue to set for a few hours before you trim the piece.

Trim the excess backing on a table saw, guiding the piece with the miter gauge, or use a sharp handsaw.

You can paint the work before or after you glue the pieces together. Before you paint, sand the lath slightly for a smoother painting surface. Practice on scrap to learn how to control the paint on the rough lath to get the effect you want. Because wood absorbs paint easily, and to avoid runs, use thick paint such as acrylic artist's paints.

First paint the ground (light yellow), house (light blue-gray) and roof (darker blue-gray). After they dry, paint the windows (yellow with red details), door (dark blue-gray with red details) and patterns (red).

When the paint is completely dry, lightly brush the entire surface with a steel-wire brush to give it an antique look.

Finally, frame the piece with lath strips **F,G** placed flush with the front surface of the picture. Lightly glue each piece and attach with 1-in. brads. Attach screw eyes and a length of picture-hanging wire to the back.

the backing and against the ground. Work from left to right with the rest of the lath, positioning the house, roof, sky, etc. Finally, glue in the two triangles.

To ensure a good glue bond, clamp the lath against the backing or place weights on the pieces. If you use weights, cover the lath with waxed

Quick & Easy

Quick & Easy 83
PROJECTS FOR OUTDOORS

FIREWOOD RACK/PLANT STAND

This project provides convenient storage for firewood (below) in the winter and converts to an outdoor plant stand (right) in the summer.

This outdoor storage project performs year-round because its purpose changes with the seasons. In the summer, it's a place to display sun-loving plants (and plants that are sensitive to the sun can be placed in the shade under the slats). In the winter, turn the stand upside down and it makes a great firewood rack.

Cedar makes a nice lightweight stand, but redwood and pressure-treated pine work equally well. To make the stand, you'll need two 8-ft.-long 2x6s, one 6-ft.-long 2x6 and one 8-ft.-long 4x4. Cut the 2x6s to length for the slats, front aprons and side aprons. Using a band saw or sabre saw, cut the notches in the two outside slats (see drawing, Slat Detail).

Using the front and side apron half-patterns in the drawing as a guide, mark the curved shapes on the

PROJECTS FOR OUTDOORS

FIREWOOD RACK/PLANT STAND

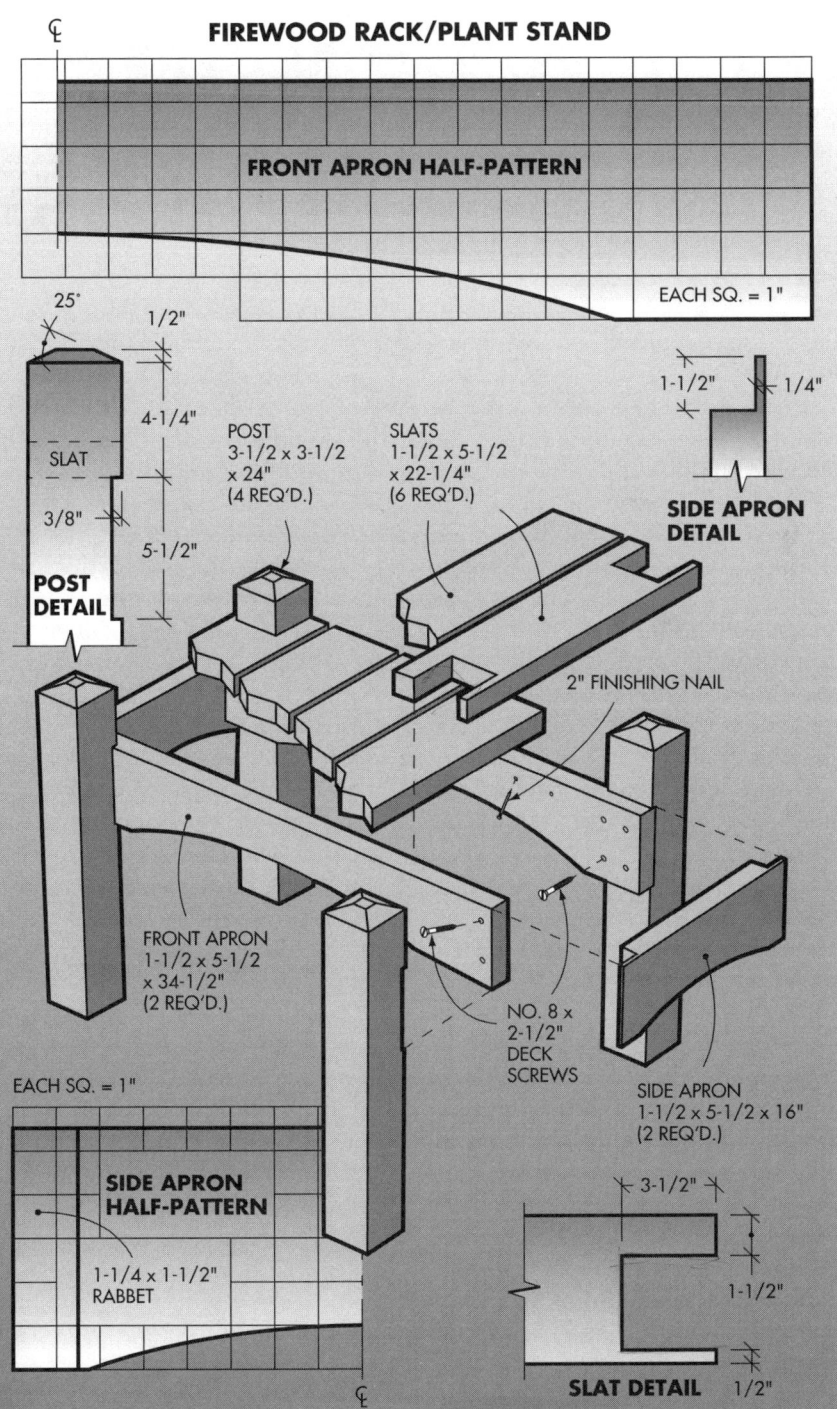

HOUSE MARKER

If you've ever been stung by the embarrassment of ringing the wrong doorbell in search of a costume party, you know how important visible house numbers are. This sign makes sure your address is in plain view for all to see no matter how long your driveway or dim your streetlights.

Except for the center panel, which is 1/4-in. plywood, the marker is made of pressure-treated pine. Begin by cutting all parts to size. Enlarge the house marker half-pattern and the post-top pattern to full size using a photocopier or draw them on graph paper with 1-in. squares. Lay out the patterns on the stock and trace around them; then cut the curves and the tapers on the ends of the posts with a sabre saw or band saw. Sand all of the edges smooth with 100-grit sandpaper.

Next, cut the grooves in the rails (see Detail 1, drawing) with a router or a table saw. Glue the center panel in the grooves with water-resistant glue such as Titebond II.

Bore counterbores and through-holes in the posts for the no. 8 x 2-1/2-in. screws. Position the center assembly between the posts and clamp; then insert an awl through the holes in the posts and mark the locations for the pilot holes in the rails.

bottom side of the aprons. The curves don't need to be cut exactly as shown in the drawing; just draw a pleasing shape with a pencil and cut it with a sabre saw. Next, cut the 1-1/4-in.-deep x 1-1/2-in.-wide rabbets in the ends of the side aprons.

Cut the legs to length; then cut the 3/8-in.-deep notches (see drawing, Post Detail) for the front aprons. The easiest way to cut the notches is with a table saw or radial arm saw fitted with a dado set. If you're limited to hand tools, make a series of 3/8-in.-deep cuts with a handsaw; then clean out the wood between the cuts with a wood chisel. Chamfer the tops and bottoms of the posts with a radial arm saw. The corners should be cut or rounded so they're not sharp. You could also use a router to round or chamfer the corners.

Begin assembly by joining the side aprons to the rabbets in the front aprons with three 2-1/2-in. deck screws (see drawing). Next, using 2-1/2-in. deck screws, attach the front aprons to the notches in the legs. Then place the outside slats in position and nail or screw them in place from the underside. This will be easier if you lay the stand upside down on scraps to hold the slats against the aprons. With the stand right side up, lay the remaining slats on the aprons so they are equally spaced; then clamp the slats in position and attach them to the aprons.

You can finish the stand with stain or exterior enamel, or let it weather to a natural gray.

PROJECTS FOR OUTDOORS

Bore the pilot holes and drive the screws.

Cut eight plugs from 1/2-in.-dia. dowel and glue them in the counterbores. For decorative purposes, the plugs protrude 1/2 in.

Finally, paint the entire assembly with exterior latex paint and add your house number.

Help guests find your home with a marker that prominently displays your house number.

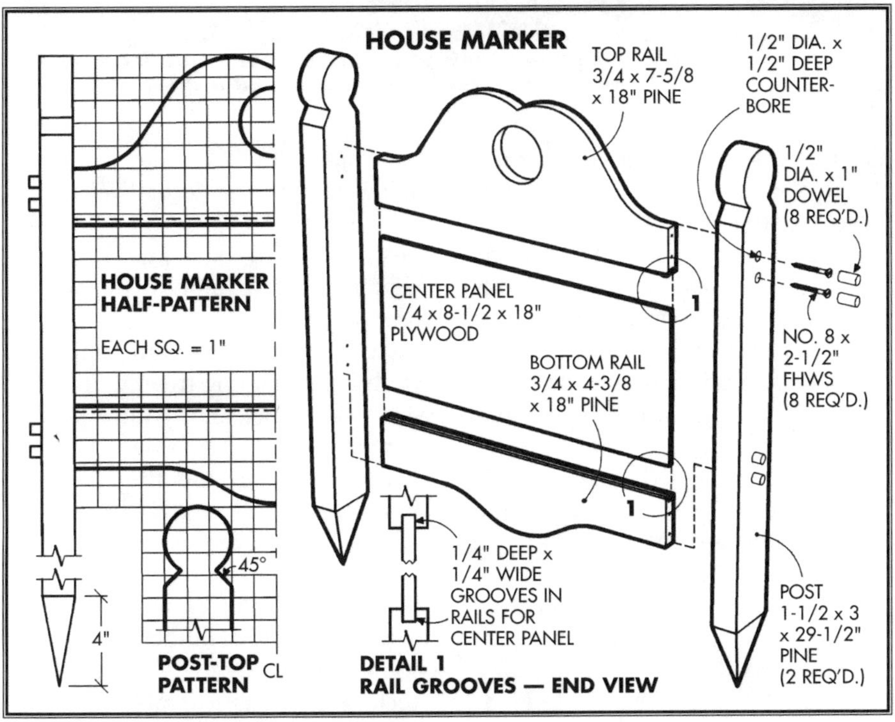

HOUSE MARKER

- TOP RAIL: 3/4 x 7-5/8 x 18" PINE
- CENTER PANEL: 1/4 x 8-1/2 x 18" PLYWOOD
- BOTTOM RAIL: 3/4 x 4-3/8 x 18" PINE
- 1/2" DIA. x 1/2" DEEP COUNTER-BORE
- 1/2" DIA. x 1" DOWEL (8 REQ'D.)
- NO. 8 x 2-1/2" FHWS (8 REQ'D.)
- POST: 1-1/2 x 3 x 29-1/2" PINE (2 REQ'D.)

HOUSE MARKER HALF-PATTERN — EACH SQ. = 1"

POST-TOP PATTERN — 45°, 4"

DETAIL 1 — RAIL GROOVES — END VIEW: 1/4" DEEP x 1/4" WIDE GROOVES IN RAILS FOR CENTER PANEL

Quick & Easy

SOUTHWEST PLANTER BOX

The only power tools you need to make this Southwest-style planter box are a sabre saw and a drill.

A planter box on a window ledge is a good place to start a small garden. The location is convenient — you can take care of the plants from the inside or outside — and the planter adds visual appeal to your house.

The planter shown has a Southwest motif, but you can easily change the details to make the box any style you like.

Almost any wood works for this project. Redwood was used here, but cedar or pine are good substitutes. If you use pine, however, plan to paint the box to prevent the wood from rotting. Although this box is designed to hold potted plants, you can fill it with dirt if you first line it with landscape fabric to keep the dirt from falling through the decorative openings. In this case, you should use pressure-treated pine and stain or paint the box to prevent the wood from deteriorating.

Cut all the pieces to the finished width before cutting them to length. Mark the corner joint with a pencil on the front, back and sides.

The corner joint fingers add strength and a decorative element to the box, but they're not essential. If you prefer, you can use simple butt joints instead. Simply subtract 1-1/2 in. from the width of the sides (provided you're using 3/4-in.-thick stock). When you assemble the box,

PROJECTS FOR OUTDOORS

Shown in Color on Page 8

nail or screw the sides between the front and the back.

Mark the decorative step pattern and the sunburst pattern on the front with a pencil. Use a sabre saw to cut the decorative cutouts in the front and the corner joints on the front, back and sides. Bore entry holes for the sabre saw blade in each element of the sunburst cutout to make it easy to start cuts.

When you've completed all the cuts, attach the bottom cleats to the sides with glue and nails. (It's best to use a water-resistant glue such as Franklin Titebond II.) Next, assemble the front, back and sides with glue and nails. Make sure the box is square; then glue and nail the bottom slats to the bottom cleats.

To complete construction, rout a 3/8-in. chamfer around the top edge and sand the entire outside of the box with 100-grit sandpaper. If you built the box of pine, finish with an exterior latex enamel. If you used redwood or cedar, apply a clear water repellent or water repellent stain.

How you mount your window box depends on how your window frame is made (see drawing). The windowsill might be wide enough so you only need to put angled blocks under the box. If the sill is too narrow, you may need to cut brackets and attach them to the side of the house. In all cases, however, you should screw the box to the mounting to prevent it from falling off.

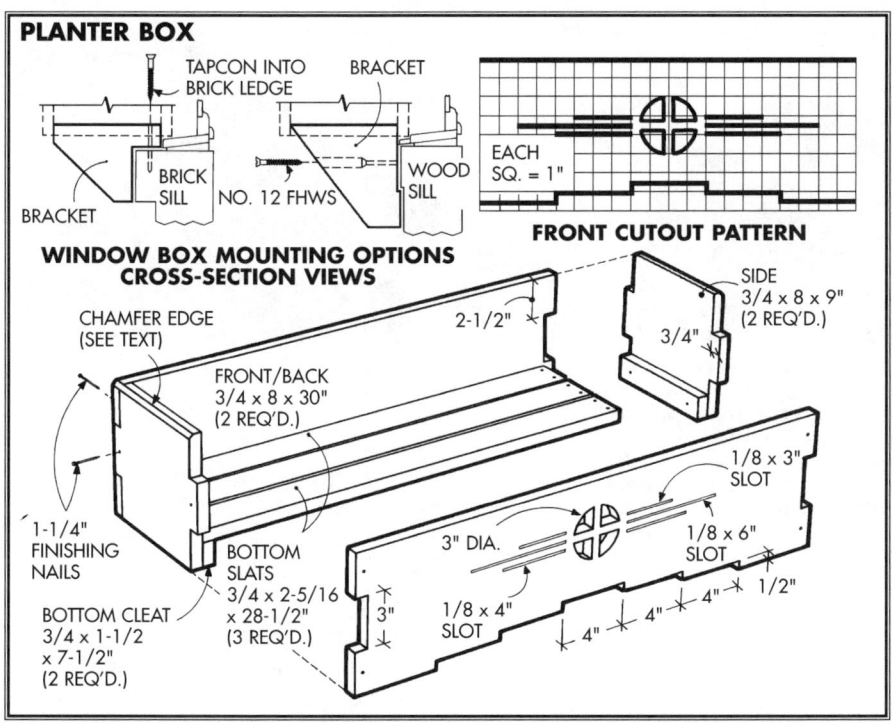

Quick & Easy

BOOT/SHOE SCRAPER

Leave mud outside where it belongs. You can make this scraper from parts that are available at any hardware store. Attach the scraper to your deck with wood screws or to concrete surfaces with Tapcon anchors.

In this country, most of us don't adhere to the sensible Japanese tradition of removing our shoes before we enter a house. We wind up paying the price when spring rain turns dirt into mud, which we track inside. Here's a way to keep your shoes on and leave the grime outside.

PROJECTS FOR OUTDOORS

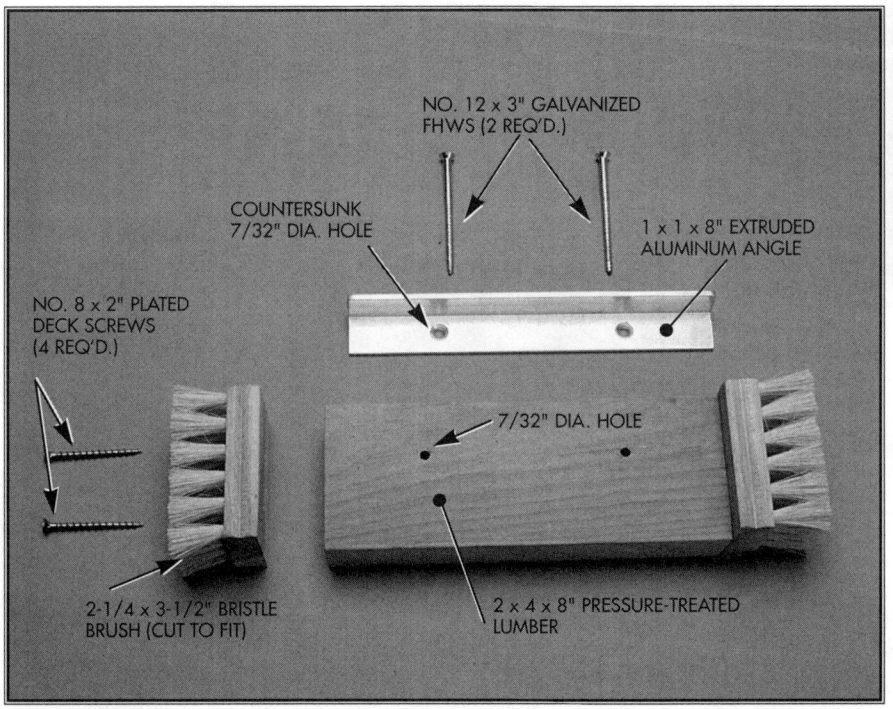

This boot scraper is the model of simplicity. Once you have the parts, it takes less than 30 minutes to make. The base is a 2x4 scrap of pressure-treated lumber. A piece of 1-in. aluminum angle provides an edge for scraping the bottom of your shoes, and a stiff-bristle wooden-handled brush cleans mud off the sides.

Cut two 3-1/2-in. pieces from the brush (the same dimension as the width of the 2x4). If the brush is too short — say 6 in. long — you can rip 1/2 in. off one edge of the base to compensate. Use a hacksaw or a table saw or miter saw with a carbide-tipped blade to cut the aluminum angle to length. Round off sharp corners and edges with a file.

Bore holes in the aluminum angle and base (about 2 in. from each edge) as shown in the photo. The holes should be slightly larger than the diameter of the screw shank to make attaching the scraper easier. Countersink the holes in the aluminum angle so that the screw heads are flush with the surface. (Use only plated or galvanized screws.)

Finally, bore two holes in each brush and screw the brushes to the ends of the base. Find a good spot near your entry door to fasten the scraper. Now get in the habit of cleaning your shoes before you step inside the house.

WOODEN DOORMAT

Build a tough mat that can stand up to snow and mud from pressure-treated pine. There's no need to stain or paint the doormat — cleaning your shoes would scrape off the finish.

Made from pressure-treated Southern pine deck boards and nylon rope, this durable doormat is the perfect remedy for snow-caked boots — stamp your feet and the snow falls between the slats. It also has tough edges so you can scrape off mud.

You'll need one 12-ft.-long 5/4x6 (1- x 5-1/2-in. actual size) deck board (or two 6-ft.-long boards) and about 16 ft. of 3/16-in.-dia. nylon rope. You can make the doormat using a portable circular saw, an electric drill, a sabre saw and a router, but a table saw or radial arm saw and a drill press will make the work go faster.

To make the 2-1/2-in.-wide slats, rip the deck board in the center, cut off the rounded edges — about 1/4 in. should do it — and then cut the slats to length. (You'll have eight slats.)

Using the grid pattern as a guide, mark the outline for the outside curves on the five front slats and cut with a sabre saw.

Using a table saw, rip the eighth slat into two 5/8-in.-wide strips for spacers. When ripping the spacer strips, place the board on the table saw so the narrow edge is on the outside of the blade, not between the blade and the fence. Then cut the strips into 18 2-1/2-in.-wide spacers. Drill 3/8-in.-dia. through-holes in the spacers (see drawing).

Lay the slats and spacers on a workbench and position them as they'll be after you've tied them together. Mark the locations of the holes on both edges of the slats with a pencil. Space the marks 1-1/2 in. apart. Using a straightedge, draw lines

PROJECTS FOR OUTDOORS

across all the slats where the holes will be. Then measure the angle and use a sliding T-bevel or angle gauge to set the table on a drill press. (The holes in the spacers can be drilled straight through, but the holes in the five front slats must be drilled at an angle.) Clamp a 2x4 block to the drill press table as a fence to ensure you drill the holes straight through the slats.

To cut the grooves in the outside slats, mount a router in a router table and cut with a 3/8-in. straight bit or round-nose (core-box) bit. If you don't have a router table, clamp the slats securely in a vise to rout the grooves.

Using the diagram in the drawing, string the nylon rope through the slats and spacers. To keep the ends from fraying, melt the ends of the rope with a torch or heat gun. Caution: Don't let melted nylon drip on your skin or clothes. Pull the rope taut; then tie a square knot. Trim the rope close to the knot and melt the ends to keep it from fraying; then press the knot into the groove.

Shown in Color on Page 9

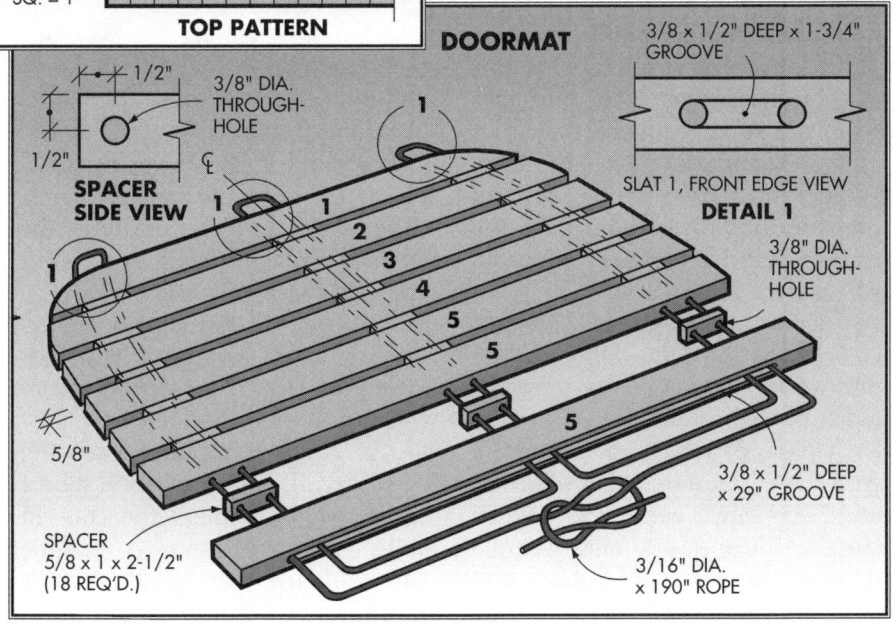

GARDEN CART

Using leftovers from a deck-building project you can build a handy cart to haul gardening tools and supplies.

f you have gardening chores to tend to, the advantages of a cart like this are obvious. You can load all of your tools and supplies in the shelves at once and save extra trips to the shed, garage or basement. Made of pressure-treated Southern pine, the cart can be painted, stained or coated with a clear preservative.

The cart requires about 32 lineal ft. of 5/4x6 Radius Edge Decking. The dimensions are nominal — the actual size of the boards is 1 in. x 5-1/2 in. Each piece of R.E.D. lumber comes with the edges rounded. You'll need one 12-ft. length cut into four equal lengths to use as side rails; two 10-ft.-long boards for the bottom end rails, bottom shelf pieces, wheel supports, top end rails, top shelf pieces and stretcher; one pressure-treated 6-ft.-long 2x4 for the uprights and feet; and one 15-in.-long piece of 1-in.-dia. dowel for the handle. The rest of your shopping list includes the wheels, carriage bolts for the axles and galvanized nails and screws.

To begin, cut all the parts to size. If you're using a radial arm saw or table saw, set up a stop block to crosscut the rails and shelf parts so they're equal. If you're crosscutting parts with a circular saw, use a square and a pencil to mark the cuts. In either case, make sure to measure and mark the parts on the boards

PROJECTS FOR OUTDOORS

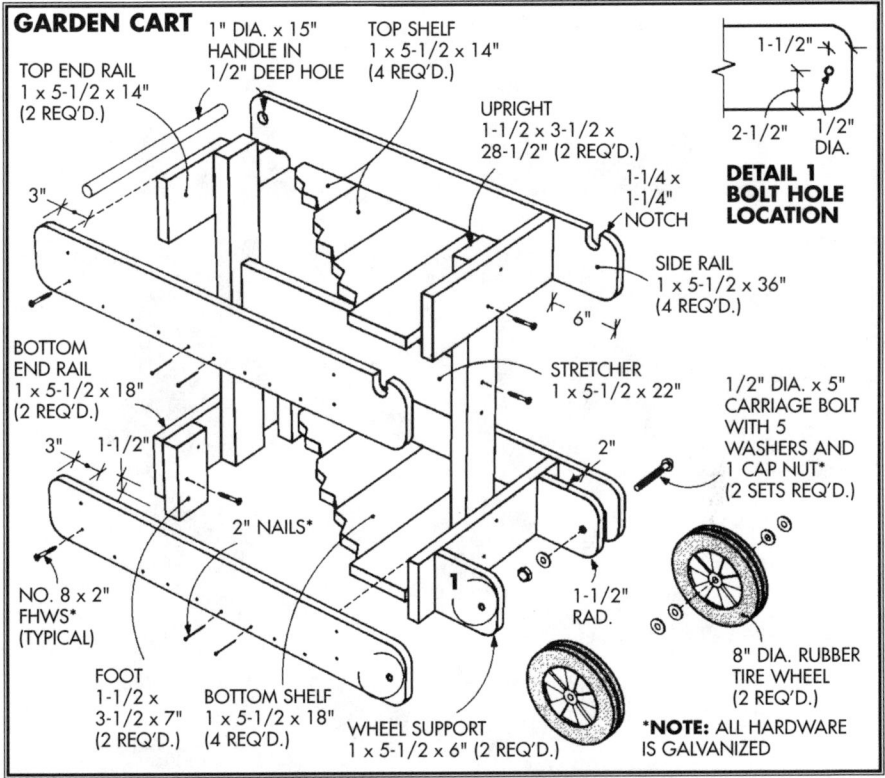

before you cut to avoid wasting any material — if you make mistakes, you may need more material than was called for above.

After you've cut the parts, lay out and mark the axle holes, handle holes and notches in the proper parts.

Center the handle holes on the 5-1/2-in.-wide board about 1 in. from the end (or position them a bit higher or lower if you prefer). The notches to hang your garden hose are optional.

Now bore the holes. Note that the handle holes are only 1/2 in. deep. A brad-point bit is best for this job. Next, cut the notches with a sabre saw and scrolling blade.

Begin assembly at the bottom by screwing the feet to one of the bottom end rails. If you have decking screws and a drill/driver with a driver bit, the job will go quickly. Otherwise, bore pilot holes for the screws first.

Next, attach the wheel supports to the other bottom end rail with screws. Be especially careful when you align the wheel supports so your axle bolts will slide in properly later. Now fasten the uprights to the bottom rails with screws. To complete the bottom assembly, attach the side rails and then nail in the shelf boards one at a time.

Repeat the procedure to assemble the top. Put the handle in place before you attach the second side rail.

Quick & Easy

FOLDING LAWN CHAIR

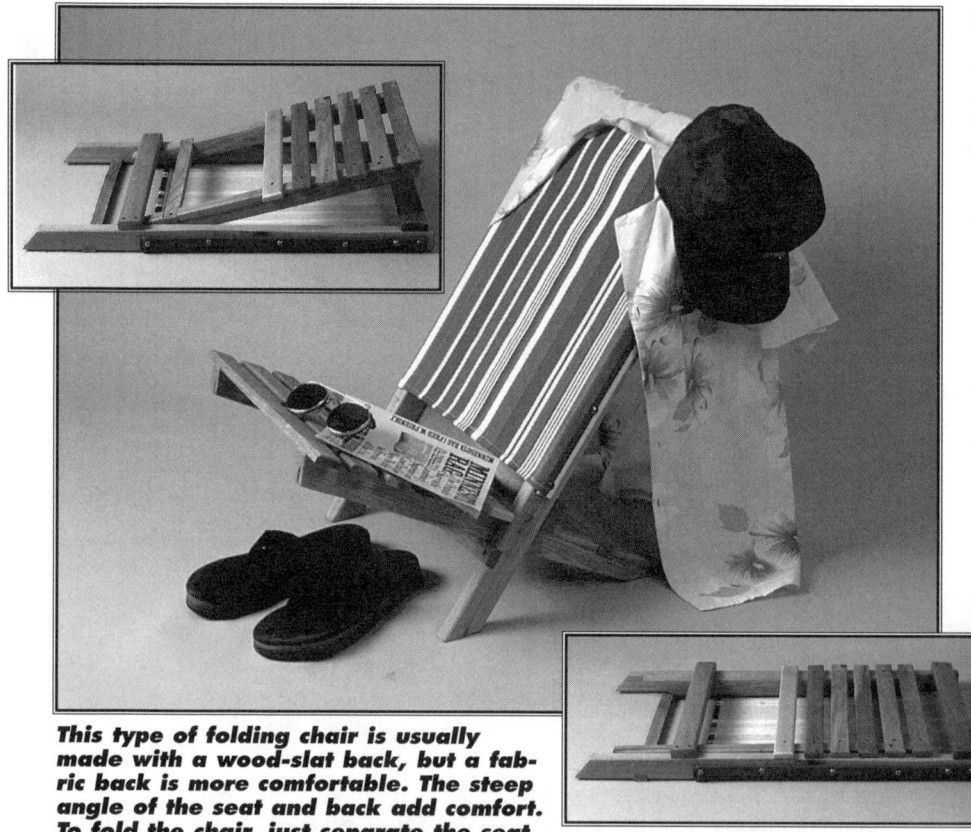

This type of folding chair is usually made with a wood-slat back, but a fabric back is more comfortable. The steep angle of the seat and back add comfort. To fold the chair, just separate the seat from the back and slip the seat between the back legs. The seat slats rest neatly against the back legs for flat storage or transportation.

This folding lawn chair is great for camping, concerts or watching TV. The one shown was made out of oak from discarded shipping pallets. The wood had to be planed to thickness with a power hand planer or a bench-top planer/jointer. If you buy stock lumber, you can avoid thickness planing.

PROJECTS FOR OUTDOORS

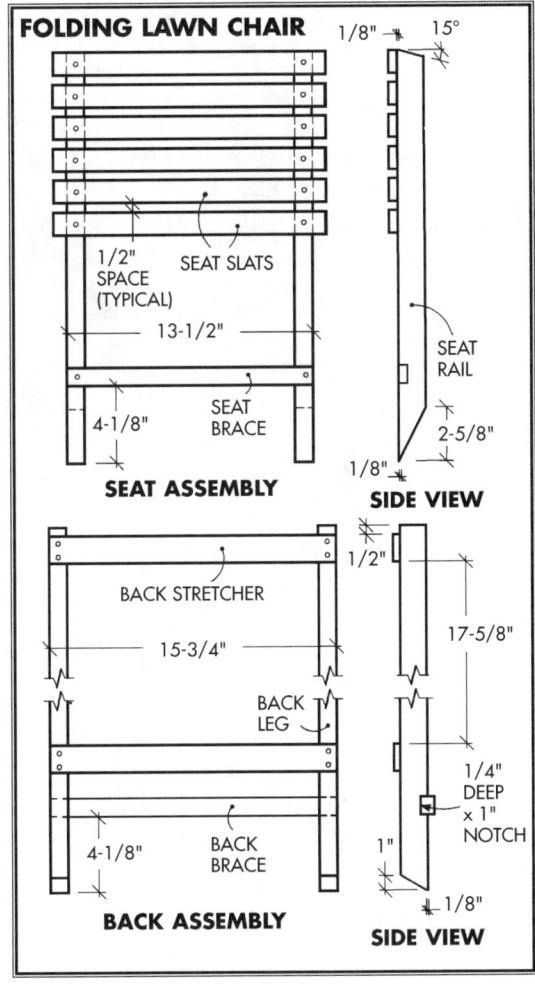

Rip all of the pieces to width first; then crosscut them to length. Cut the notches in the back legs and in the seat legs to accept the braces. Use a dado blade on a radial arm saw and make two passes for each notch. Clamp stop blocks to the saw fence on both sides of the leg so the notches are the same width.

With all the pieces cut to size, use a router and a 1/4-in. rounding over bit to round all four edges of the back legs. Round over just the bottom edges of the seat legs as well, and round the stretchers and the top edges of the seat slats.

Next, bore countersinks and clearance holes in the seat slats and in both braces and both stretchers. Use a drill press or a hand-held drill. If you're building the chair out of oak or any hard wood, don't forget to drill pilot holes into the legs for the screws.

Cut the ends of the legs as shown in the drawing. You can fine-tune the angles after assembly so that the legs rest securely on the ground.

Sand all the parts with 120-grit sandpaper; then assemble. Glue the braces into the notches; then drive 1-in. galvanized screws. Attach the stretchers to the back legs, making sure the assembly is square. Next, attach all the seat slats to the seat assembly.

Spray the assemblies with clear lacquer; then make the fabric back. The chair shown has a canvas back, but you can substitute any suitable fabric. Lay out your fabric to see how much it stretches and adjust the dimensions if necessary before stitching the hems and sleeves. Cut the sticks to fit in the sleeves. To install the fabric back, tack one side to a leg top

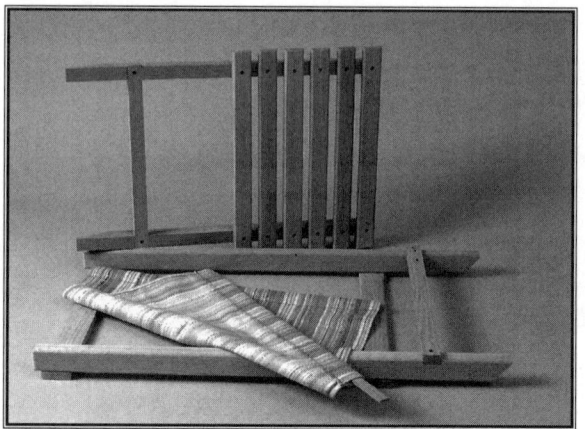

and bottom; then tack the other side at the top and at the bottom. Add the center tack on each side; then fill in the remaining tacks.

The fabric back is hemmed on top and bottom and sleeves are sewn in the sides to accept the wood sticks. Attach the fabric with upholstery nails through the sticks into the back legs.

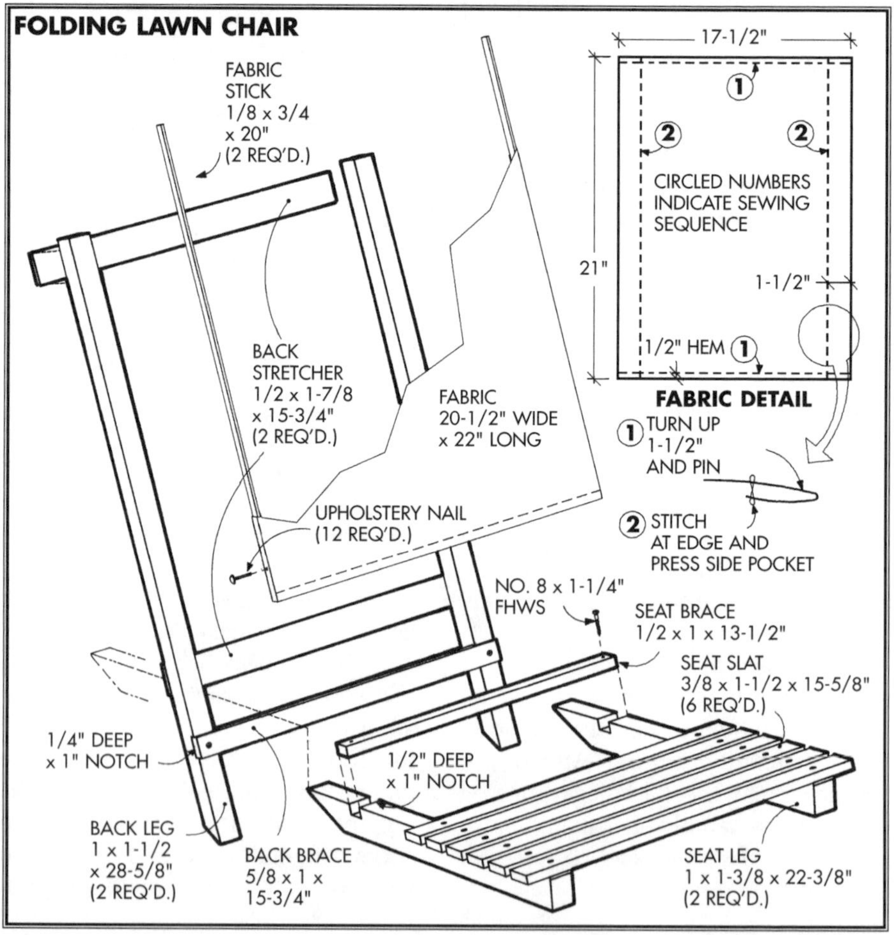

FOLDING LAWN CHAIR

FABRIC STICK
1/8 x 3/4 x 20"
(2 REQ'D.)

BACK STRETCHER
1/2 x 1-7/8 x 15-3/4"
(2 REQ'D.)

FABRIC
20-1/2" WIDE x 22" LONG

UPHOLSTERY NAIL
(12 REQ'D.)

NO. 8 x 1-1/4" FHWS

1/4" DEEP x 1" NOTCH

1/2" DEEP x 1" NOTCH

BACK LEG
1 x 1-1/2 x 28-5/8"
(2 REQ'D.)

BACK BRACE
5/8 x 1 x 15-3/4"

SEAT BRACE
1/2 x 1 x 13-1/2"

SEAT SLAT
3/8 x 1-1/2 x 15-5/8"
(6 REQ'D.)

SEAT LEG
1 x 1-3/8 x 22-3/8"
(2 REQ'D.)

FABRIC DETAIL

17-1/2"

21"

1-1/2"

1/2" HEM ①

CIRCLED NUMBERS INDICATE SEWING SEQUENCE

① TURN UP 1-1/2" AND PIN

② STITCH AT EDGE AND PRESS SIDE POCKET

PROJECTS FOR OUTDOORS

BERRY BOX

Shown in Color on Page 9

The box provides a convenient way to transport your garden goodies. A cutting board is stored in a recess beneath the plywood bottom. The box can easily be built without the recess if you prefer.

This box looks like a tool caddie, but it was designed for carrying vegetables, berries and flowers from the garden. A built-in cutting board makes serving convenient.

Start by ripping a piece of 1x4 pine (3/4 x 3-1/2 in. actual size) to 3-3/8 in. wide. Cut two 22-1/2-in. lengths for the sides and two 13-3/8-in. lengths for the ends. Mark the dovetail joints on the sides (see drawing, Joint Detail, p. 101) and cut with a band saw, a fine-tooth backsaw or a scroll saw.

Fit the sides to the ends and trace around the cut dovetails (photo 2, p. 100). It's a good idea to number the pieces so you'll be sure to join the right ones together later. For a tight fit, cut the waste between the half pins well inside the pencil lines (photo 3); you can always shave off the extra wood. Remove the waste with a chisel (photo 4) and assemble the sides and ends without glue to check the fit of the dovetail. Use a sharp chisel to pare and fit the joint if necessary.

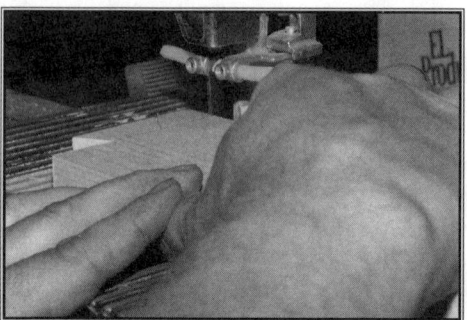

1 Cut the dovetail on a band saw with a fine-tooth 1/4-in.-wide blade.

2 Trace the tail directly onto the end of the end piece to mark the half pins. Use a combination square to extend the layout lines down the face.

3 Mark the depth of the half pins; then cut them with a tenon saw or backsaw as shown. Be careful not to cut below the layout line.

Mark the 1/4- x 1/4-in. groove in the sides and ends for the lauan plywood bottom and cut with a router and a 1/4-in. straight mortising bit. The groove should not extend all the way to the edge of the end pieces nor through the dovetail in the side pieces or it will show when the pieces are joined (see drawing).

Using a utility knife, cut the lauan plywood bottom to size and cut a 1/4- x 1/4-in. notch in each corner to fit around the stopped groove. Join all the pieces with glue and clamp until the glue dries.

Make a template for the divider using the half-pattern in the drawing. Enlarge the half-pattern on a photocopier or draw it on graph paper. Trace the template onto a 1x8 (3/4 x 7-1/4 in. actual size) and cut with a coping saw, scroll saw or sabre saw. Sand the divider smooth and round over the edges of the handle with a router.

The divider is attached to the ends with glue and 1-5/8-in. drywall screws. Drill two pilot holes and two counterbores in the center of each piece and install the divider. (You can also use four small wood screws to attach the bottom to the divider until the glue dries.) Cover the drywall screws with 3/8-in.-dia. dowels.

Sand the entire box with 120-grit sandpaper; then finish with paint or stain and two coats of polyurethane.

Make the cutting board from a tight-grained hard wood (maple is ideal) to keep bacteria from growing in the wood. It's easiest to make the cutting board from one piece of wood, but you can glue narrow

PROJECTS FOR OUTDOORS

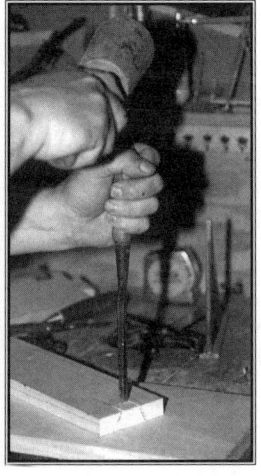

4 With the bevel side of the chisel facing the end of the board, remove the waste from beneath the half pins. To avoid tearing the wood on the opposite side, chisel about halfway down and then turn the board over to remove the rest of the waste.

5 After routing the grooves in the sides and cutting the bottom, assemble the box with glue. Install the divider and cover the counterbored screws with plugs.

pieces together if necessary.

Cut the handle with a sabre saw, scroll saw or router (see Detail 1). Round the four corners of the board; then round over all of the edges with a router. Sand the entire board smooth with 150-grit sandpaper. Leave the board unfinished.

Finally, install the four plastic screen retainers (available at hardware stores) that hold the cutting board in its recess under the box bottom.

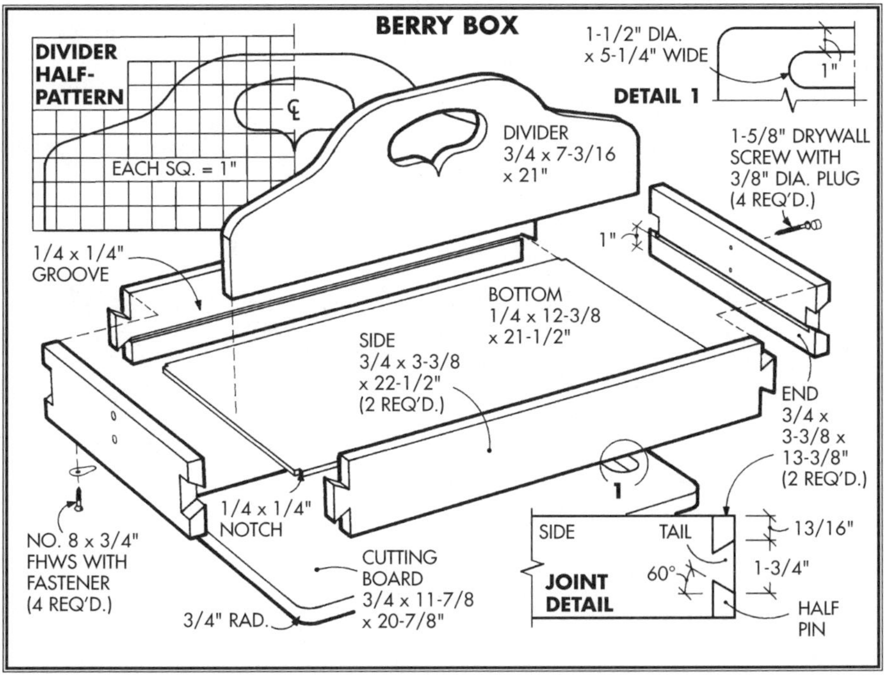

BERRY BOX

- DIVIDER HALF-PATTERN — EACH SQ. = 1"
- DIVIDER 3/4 x 7-3/16 x 21"
- 1-1/2" DIA. x 5-1/4" WIDE
- DETAIL 1 — 1"
- 1-5/8" DRYWALL SCREW WITH 3/8" DIA. PLUG (4 REQ'D.)
- 1/4 x 1/4" GROOVE
- BOTTOM 1/4 x 12-3/8 x 21-1/2"
- SIDE 3/4 x 3-3/8 x 22-1/2" (2 REQ'D.)
- END 3/4 x 3-3/8 x 13-3/8" (2 REQ'D.)
- 1/4 x 1/4" NOTCH
- NO. 8 x 3/4" FHWS WITH FASTENER (4 REQ'D.)
- 3/4" RAD.
- CUTTING BOARD 3/4 x 11-7/8 x 20-7/8"
- JOINT DETAIL: SIDE, TAIL, 60°, 13/16", 1-3/4", HALF PIN

Quick & Easy

Quick & Easy 103

KIDS' STUFF

TOY CATAPULT

Squeeze the clothespin open and the rubber band-powered arm throws the lightweight missile several feet.

n spite of our best efforts to promote peace, children have always enjoyed fighting imaginary wars. Entertain young mercenaries with this replica of an ancient military catapult, which hurls a pingpong ball a few feet. No matter how murderous the intent of the young soldier operating it, the catapult is safe — the lightweight ball won't cause any casualties.

The base, sides and wheels are made out of 7/8-in.-thick birch scrap

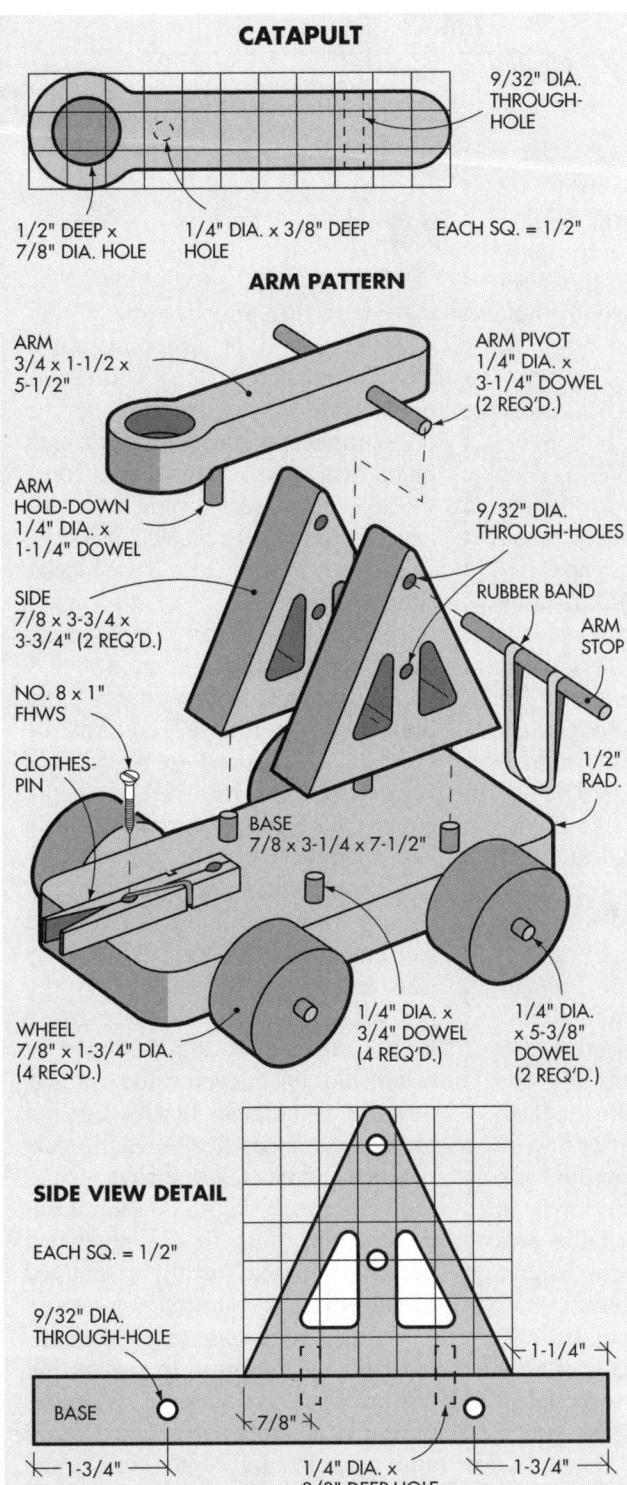

(the arm is 3/4 in. thick), but 3/4-in.-thick pine or any other wood will work. You can cut the wheels with a hole saw or purchase them ready-made. Use 1/4-in. dowels for the axles, arm pivot, arm stop and arm hold-down. The trigger is a spring clothespin.

First, enlarge the arm and side patterns to full size on a photocopier, or draw them full size on graph paper. Trace the patterns on your stock; then make the outside cuts with a band saw.

Use the patterns to locate the cutouts in the sides. Drill 1/4-in.-dia. holes in each corner; then complete the cutouts with a scroll saw or coping saw. Drill 9/32-in.-dia. holes in the sides for the arm pivot and the arm stop.

Cut out the base and bore 9/32-in.-dia. through-holes for the wheel axles. Clamp the base on a drill press table while drilling to ensure the holes are true. Next, bore four 1/4-in.-dia. x 3/8-in.-deep holes for the dowels that attach the base to the sides. Using dowel centers, transfer the hole centers to the sides and bore the holes.

Bore a 1/4-in.-deep x 7/8-in.-dia. hole in the arm with a flat-bottom bit; then bore a 1/4-in.-dia. x 3/8-in.-deep hole for the arm hold-down. Round over the outside edges of all the pieces using a block plane or sandpaper.

Insert 1/4-in.-dia. x 5-3/8-in. dowels through the base and attach the wheels with a dab of glue. (Make sure you don't glue the dowels to the base.) The wheels should have about 1/16 in. clearance from the sides of the base.

Attach the sides to the base with 1/4-in. dowels and glue. Install the arm hold-down in the arm; then install the arm-pivot and arm-stop dowels.

To find the position for the clothespin, place a 1-in. flathead wood screw or a drywall screw through the spring and clip the clothespin to the hold-down. Push the arm tight against the base and let the screw mark the spot on the base; then screw the clothespin down. (If the clothespin won't hold the arm with the rubber band attached, move the clothespin slightly forward.)

Finally, slip a 1/8- x 3-in. (no. 32) rubber band around the arm stop and over the arm (it will rest against the arm hold-down) and you're ready to go into battle.

It's easy to turn your favorite photograph, postcard or wrapping paper into a puzzle to challenge youngsters or decorate a living room shelf. The only supplies you need are white craft glue, clear acrylic finish and some wood — inexpensive pine or scraps left over from other projects will do.

Before you start cutting the blocks, choose six prints — one for each block side. Choose prints with a sturdy paper backing — avoid flimsy paper and very shiny prints. Color photocopies work well and can be enlarged or reduced to the size of your choice. You may want to keep a copy of each print intact to use as a key when solving the puzzle.

Cut out each print the size you want the assembled puzzle to be. You can make any number of blocks any size and configuration to suit the print. The blocks shown are made from 3-in.-thick stock (resulting in six square blocks), but you could use 2x4s to make rectangular blocks. Cut the blocks a uniform size — sharp, perpendicular cuts are imperative — and sand the rough edges. Be careful not to sand too much or the edges will become rounded and the assembled puzzle will look distorted.

Arrange the blocks to suit the configuration of the print. To ensure that the print will be centered when the puzzle is assembled, draw a vertical and a horizontal centerline on the

KIDS' STUFF

DECOUPAGE PUZZLE BLOCKS

Shown in Color on Page 10

ABOVE: Puzzle blocks date back to the 18th century. These blocks were made with old-fashioned gift wrap to give them an antique look.

LEFT: Supplies you'll need include wood blocks, a ruler, a hobby knife, white glue, a glue spreader (or a brush) and two copies of each print — one to cut up and one to use as a key when solving the puzzle.

back of the print. Measure out from the center and divide the print into pieces the same size as the blocks.

Using a hobby knife, carefully cut the print into pieces; then glue each piece to a block with a good-quality white craft glue. (You may need to thin the glue with a drop of water, but don't add more than a drop or the water will damage the print.) Cover the remaining block sides in the same manner. Finally, apply a clear acrylic finish to protect the puzzle pieces. Any clear acrylic sealer — brush on or spray — will do.

Quick & Easy

ALPHABET SHELF

Alphabet blocks joined with glue and dowels make friendly shelf brackets. Use two screws to attach the hanger brackets to the shelf.

This easy-to-make shelf incorporates store-bought alphabet blocks glued and doweled together to make shelf brackets, which adds an inexpensive decorative touch. If you prefer, you can cut your own blocks for the brackets and paint them yourself.

The important part of this project is to bore the dowel holes accurately. Start by laying out the blocks on a table the way you plan to assemble them. Find and mark the center of the block sides that accept the 1/4-in. dowels (see drawing, opposite). Bore through-holes in six of the blocks and bore a little more than halfway through the others. Use a drill press to ensure the holes align for easy insertion of the dowels.

If you don't have a drill press, use a drill bit slightly larger than 1/4 in. (9/32 or 5/16) to help the dowels pass through the holes and keep the blocks aligned. Put glue on the block

KIDS' STUFF

sides and in the dowel holes, and assemble the horizontal rows of blocks with the 1/4-in. dowels.

Now mark and bore the 1/8-in.-dia. holes. (You'll bore through the 1/4-in. dowels.) Again, make the holes slightly larger if you're drilling by hand. Fasten the rows to each other with glue and dowels.

Cut your shelf to size; then sand and paint it. Use a drill to counterbore the screw holes in the top of the shelf. (The counterbores accept the wood buttons.) Lay the shelf and brackets in position and drill through the counterbores into the top of the blocks with a 3/32-in. bit. This creates the proper size pilot hole for no. 8 x 1-1/2-in. screws. Glue and screw the shelf to the brackets and add painted buttons. All that's left is to hang the shelf with the appropriate wall anchors.

Shown in Color on Page 10

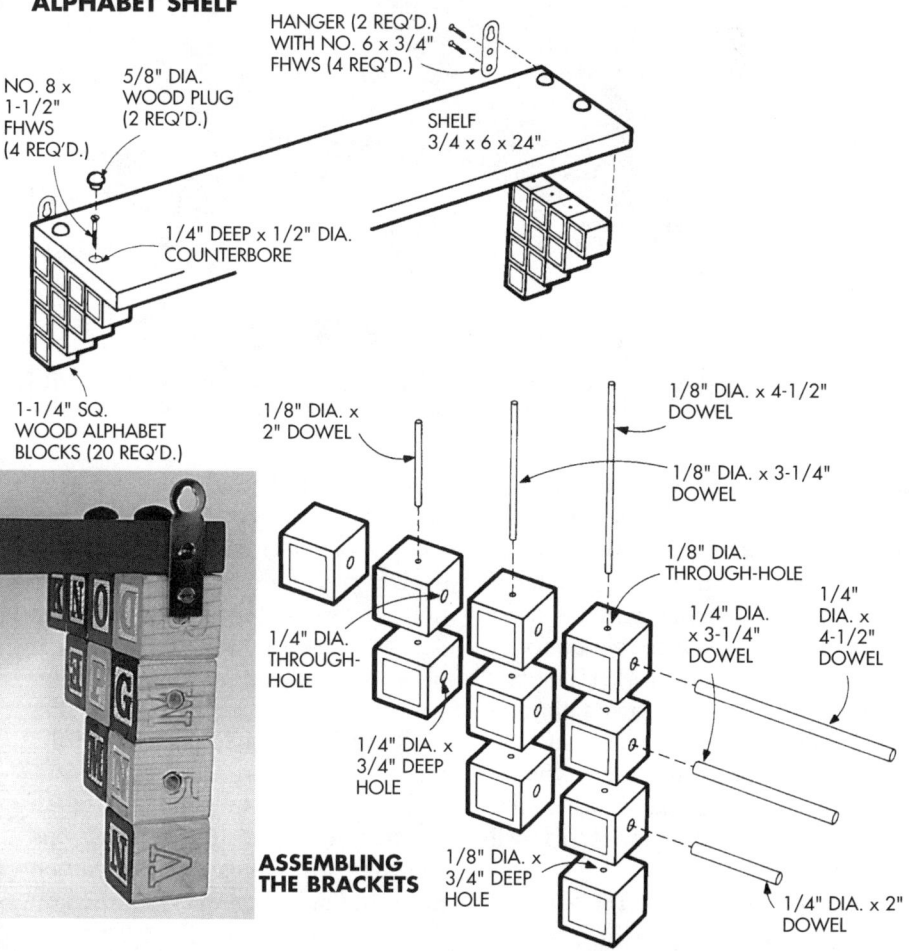

ALPHABET SHELF

Quick & Easy

BEWILDERING BLOCKS

Challenge children (and adults) with a perplexing puzzle that's easy to make.

Children and adults will be challenged by this six-piece brainteaser. You can build it from scraps and apply a clear finish, stain or paint.

The only material you need to make the puzzle is a couple of board feet of 1-1/2-in.-thick stock. (The puzzle shown is made of poplar, but any wood will work.) Power tools such as a band saw, table saw, sabre saw or radial arm saw make cutting the notches easier, but hand tools will work as well.

Begin by cutting six 1-1/2- x 1-1/2- x 8-in. blocks. Then lay out the notches as shown in the drawing. You can use several methods to cut the notches. If you use a table saw to cut the notches, raise the blade so it protrudes 3/4 in. above the table. Then, using a plywood crosscutting jig or a miter gauge with an auxiliary extension fence, make multiple passes over the blade to cut each notch.

If all you have are hand tools, use a backsaw in a miter box to make the crosscuts on the layout lines; then make multiple cuts between the lay-

KIDS' STUFF

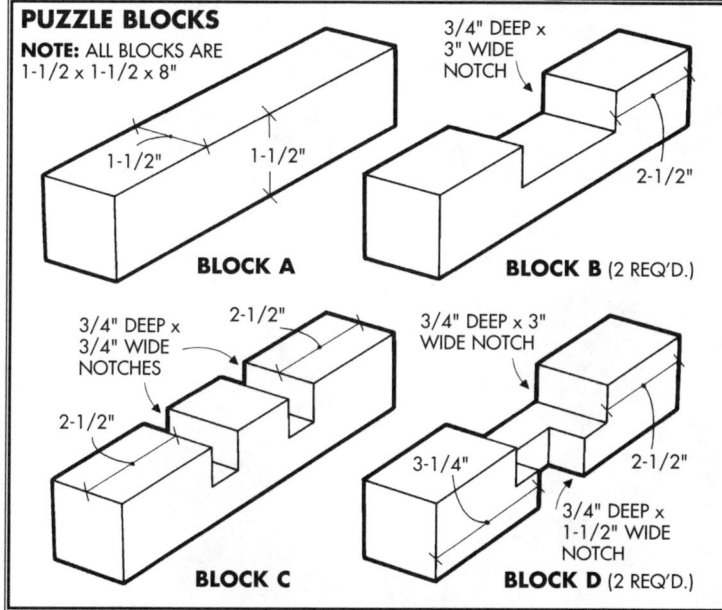

To solve the puzzle, follow the steps in the illustration below. After assembling blocks B and C, add blocks D as shown. When block A is added, the puzzle is symmetrical.

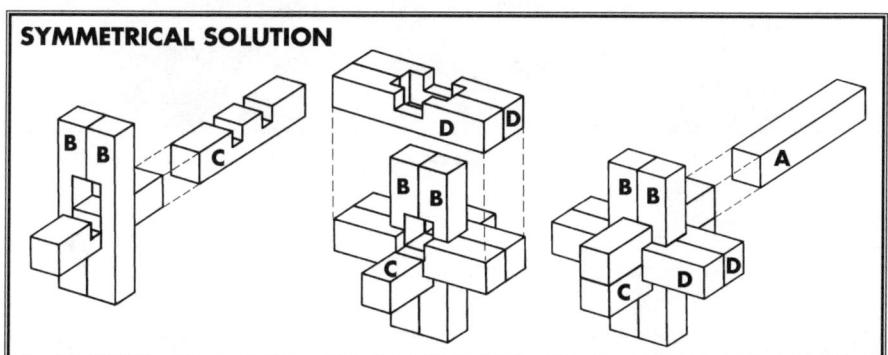

out lines and remove the waste with a sharp 3/4-in.-wide chisel.

Regardless of the method you use, cut the larger notch in block **D** first, then lay out and cut the smaller notch. Sand each block smooth with 180-grit sandpaper and a sanding block.

Assemble the puzzle to check the fit of the pieces — they should slip into place easily. If the fit is too snug, enlarge the notches by sanding.

The puzzle shown in the photo is finished with oil, but you could use an oil-base enamel. If you decide to use enamel, make sure the fit of the pieces is loose enough to compensate for the thickness of the paint.

RUBBER BAND BLOCK TOY

This block toy will entertain kids of all ages.

A rubber band makes this simple block toy flexible, so it can be arranged in a variety of configurations. All you need to make the toy is a scrap of wood, a 1/8-in.-dia. dowel, a long rubber band, a drill and a table saw.

It doesn't matter what kind of wood you make the toy out of — use whatever you have on hand. Begin by crosscutting a 7/8- x 1-3/4- x 12-in. strip. (Although you need only about 6 in. of stock to make the blocks, it is unsafe to work with pieces smaller than 12 in. on a table saw.)

The first step is to cut a 1/8-in.-wide x 1/2-in.-deep kerf that runs the length of the block in the middle of each 7/8-in. side. (See Cutting Sequence, opposite.) Position the stock against the saw fence and use a pushstick to pass it over the blade.

Now you need to crosscut six kerfs in each side running perpendicular to the lengthwise kerfs. Space the kerfs 7/8 in. apart. (This allows for 1/8 in. of waste when you cut the blocks apart.) Use a miter gauge to guide the work.

Next, bore 3/16-in.-dia. through-holes at each intersection of the perpendicular kerfs. Then cut the six blocks apart using a table saw and a miter gauge.

Paint or stain the blocks. When they're dry, thread a single rubber band through the blocks and insert a 1/8-in.-dia. x 7/8-in.-long dowel at each end to hold the rubber band in place.

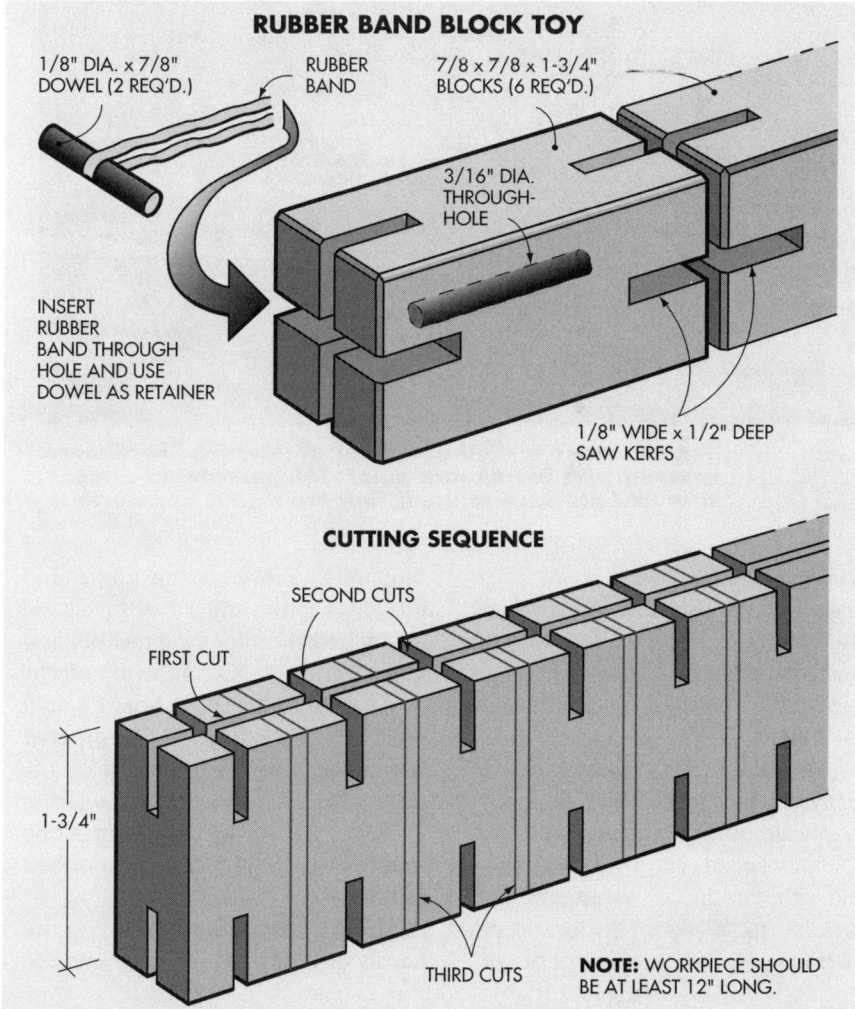

SCHOOLHOUSE BLACKBOARD

You can make a chalkboard out of tempered hardboard covered with blackboard paint. The paint takes some care and patience to apply, but the results are worth it.

A custom-designed blackboard is an educational and fun addition to any kid's room. For less than $50 you can construct a scaled-down version of the old-fashioned schoolhouse blackboard.

The construction procedure can be divided into three basic steps: cutting, assembling and painting. A table saw speeds cutting, but a hand-held circular saw or sabre saw will work. A radial arm saw or power miter saw makes quick work of cutting miter joints on the frame and moldings, but a miter box (available at any home center for a few dollars) and a backsaw will do the job nicely.

To make the blackboard you'll need one 3- x 4-ft. sheet of tempered hardboard, one 14-ft. length of 1x4 pine (3/4 x 3-1/2 in. actual size), one 14-ft. length of 1/2- x 3/4-in. shoe molding and one 5-ft. length of bed molding.

Begin construction by cutting the hardboard **A** to size. Next, cut the

KIDS' STUFF

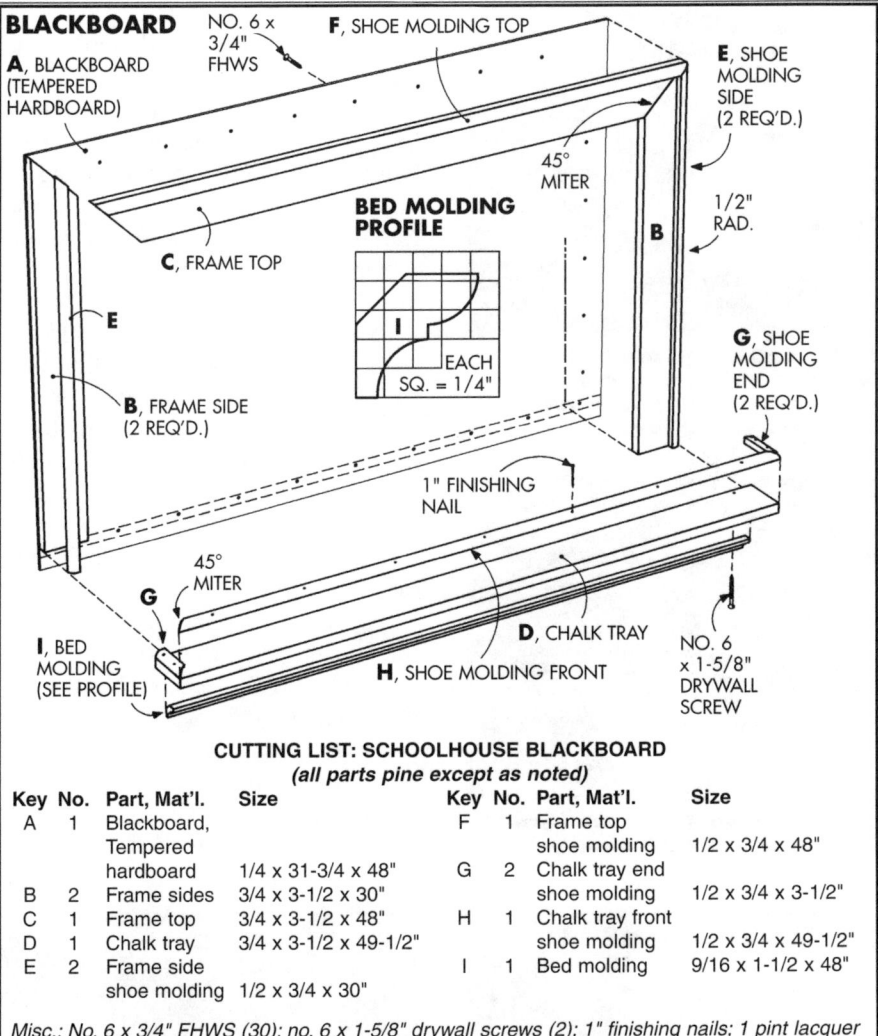

CUTTING LIST: SCHOOLHOUSE BLACKBOARD
(all parts pine except as noted)

Key	No.	Part, Mat'l.	Size
A	1	Blackboard, Tempered hardboard	1/4 x 31-3/4 x 48"
B	2	Frame sides	3/4 x 3-1/2 x 30"
C	1	Frame top	3/4 x 3-1/2 x 48"
D	1	Chalk tray	3/4 x 3-1/2 x 49-1/2"
E	2	Frame side shoe molding	1/2 x 3/4 x 30"
F	1	Frame top shoe molding	1/2 x 3/4 x 48"
G	2	Chalk tray end shoe molding	1/2 x 3/4 x 3-1/2"
H	1	Chalk tray front shoe molding	1/2 x 3/4 x 49-1/2"
I	1	Bed molding	9/16 x 1-1/2 x 48"

Misc.: No. 6 x 3/4" FHWS (30); no. 6 x 1-5/8" drywall screws (2); 1" finishing nails; 1 pint lacquer or shellac; 1 quart blackboard paint.

1x4 pine into four pieces to make the blackboard frame: two 30-in. pieces for the sides **B**, one 48-in. piece for the top **C** and one 49-1/2-in. piece for the chalk tray **D**. Miter the top piece and the top end of each side piece (photo 1, p. 116). Next, cut the shoe molding parts **E** through **H**. Miter the moldings as shown in the drawing. Finally, cut the bed molding **I** to length.

After the wood has been cut to the correct measurements, you're ready to begin assembly. First, glue one frame side **A** to the hardboard (photo 2),

1 The 1x4 frame can be butt-joined or mitered. A radial arm saw set for a 45-degree cut miters a frame piece.

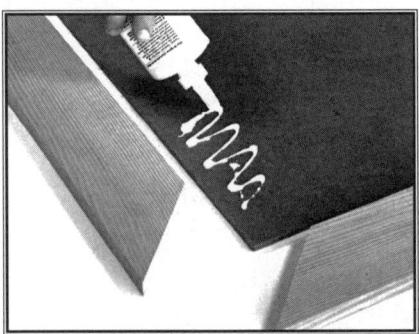

2 Squeeze glue onto the hardboard and spread it evenly.

aligning the edge of the wood with the edge of the hardboard. Use clamps to keep the parts aligned. Glue the frame top **B** to the hardboard next, followed by the other frame side **A**. Now turn the entire section facedown on a padded surface and secure the frame with 3/4-in. flathead wood screws spaced about 5 in. apart (photo 3). Remove the clamps.

Attach the shoe molding **E,F** to the frame with glue and 1-in. finishing nails. Attach shoe molding **G,H** to the chalk tray the same way. Next, attach the chalk tray **D** as shown in photo 5. For extra strength, add a 1-5/8-in. drywall screw or flathead wood screw through the bottom of the chalk tray into the end of each side frame.

For a professional-looking job, set the finishing nails that hold the molding in place with a nail set. Next, fill all the nail holes and any gaps with wood putty and allow it to dry. After the putty is dry, sand all wood surfaces, particularly the edges. Remove all traces of sawdust with a tack cloth

3 Attach the frame to the hardboard by driving screws through the back of the hardboard into the frame.

4 Next, miter the shoe molding to fit and glue and nail it to the frame.

KIDS' STUFF

(photo 6). Fill the gaps between the hardboard and the frame (photo 7).

Now you're ready to begin painting. First, apply one coat of lacquer or shellac to seal the hardboard. While you're waiting for the lacquer to dry, apply a primer coat to the pine frame. After the lacquer has dried completely (about 24 hours), apply the blackboard paint. (Blackboard slating was used on the project shown — look for it in local paint stores.) Follow the instructions on the can. Apply one coat and wait 12 hours for it to dry; then apply a second coat, slightly thinned with 1 part mineral spirits to 4 parts slating. Wait 12 hours for this coat to dry as well; then apply another thinned coat.

Paint the frame with two coats of semigloss interior paint and decorate it as you wish. Finally, attach the blackboard to wall studs (or use appropriate wall anchors), securing it at the top and bottom of the frame. Then cover the exposed hardboard at the bottom with the bed molding. **I**

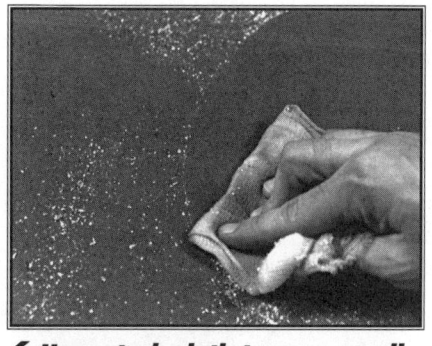

6 *Use a tack cloth to remove all dust before applying the blackboard slating.*

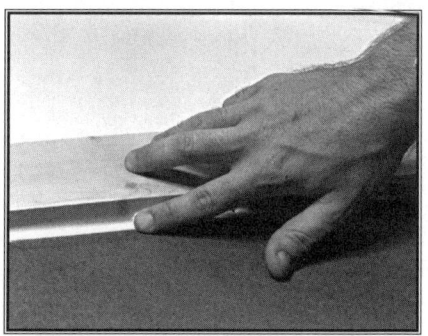

7 *Caulk the frame-hardboard joint to keep chalk dust from building up in the crevice.*

5 *Secure the chalk tray by gluing and screwing it to the hardboard.*

8 *Seal the hardboard with lacquer; then apply blackboard slating.*

NOTES

Your Choice of
One of These
4 Popular
Project Plans

FREE Gift!

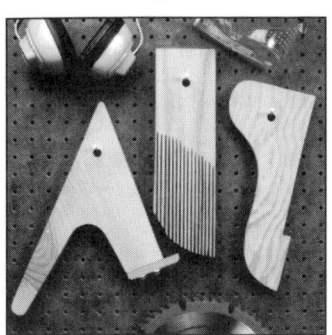

Five Shop Jigs
WBH2095 $12.95

Red Wagon
WBH2052 $12.95

Five For the Birds
WBHBF5 $14.95

Freestanding Backyard Deck
WBH2070 $12.95

**MasterCard, VISA, Discover and American Express
Credit Card Orders Call Toll-Free 1-800-678-8025**

Use This Form to Order Your Free Project Plans and to Purchase Other WORKBENCH Plans or Books

Item #	Description	Qty.	Price
	(Your Choice)	1	FREE
	Total for Books and Products		
	Shipping and Handling		$3.00
	Missouri Residents Add 6% tax, Iowa Residents 5%		
	Total Enclosed		

Name
Address
City
State and Zip

Place order form in envelope and mail to:
WORKBENCH Books and Products, Dept B95
P.O. Box 11230
Des Moines, IA 50340